For Wacco and David
and all our Dear Friends

THE FIRESIGN THEATRE'S
Big Book Of Plays

Straight Arrow Books

Acknowledgements
Our appreciation to Bill Logan of Yale University for an unusual transcript of "Dwarf." Our thanks to the many photographers who have contributed to this book, including: John Rose, Liz Plum, Dr. W. Deadjellie, Lee Greathouse, Lou Liserani, Marv Lyons, Josh Weiner, Dean Goodhill, Mark Gottlieb, Teddy Photographer, A. Kodak, Pix Bergman, and Film Proctor.

Designed by Jon Goodchild. Cover: Virginia Clive-Smith.

Citations
   P. 16–17:/quotes from an interview with David Reitman in *Rock* Magazine, and from an interview with Tony Vellela in *Go* Magazine.
   P. 21:/From interviews with Michael Ross in *Creem*, and Ernest Leogrand in the *N.Y. Daily News*.
   P. 37:/From interviews with John Carpenter in the *L.A. Free Press*, and with representatives of the San Diego *Door*.
   P. 59:/From interviews with Michael Ross in *Creem*, and David Reitman in *Rock*.
   P. 99–101:/The Firesign Theatre, as transcribed by Richard Hill for *Rolling Stone*.

Library of Congress Catalog Card No: 72/79024
SBN: 0/87932/027/3 (paperbound)
0/87932/028/1 (casebound)

First Printing

Straight Arrow Books, 625 Third Street, San Francisco, CA 94107

Distributed by: Quick Fox Inc, 33 West 60th Street, NY 10023
Printed by: Levison McNally, Reno, USA

Contents

A Forward into The Past

*In which Uncle Petey writes a little poem
dedicated to the boys and girls
in honor of the next five years*

Four pigfishes swimming bravely
In the ocean's hollow heart
Coming to the surface to warn of the storm
Floating on the surface to warm in the sun.
I would rather be a laughing fish than the
President Of The Universe; but
If I must be both to float,
Then I will hollow out a boat from gentle bamboo
And set it out to sail upon the earth,
Among the stars
And its banner shall be a sign of fire
And its kitchen will open from noon to noon,
And none shall go away unfull,
Even if we have to eat the moon.

THE FIRESIGN THEATRE

A Straight, Forward Look At The Firesign Theatre

A Straight, Forward Look At The Firesign Theatre

I have been an active professor here at SSU in Wisconsin since March, 1968. I was first made aware of the existence of the so-called Firesign Theatre when one of my more headstrong pupils handed in a lengthy and very complicated term paper which compared a work titled "Don't Squash That Dwarf, Hand Me The Pliers" with Wilheim Reich III's controversial study "Consciousness Three."

Affixed as a kind of Appendix to this unique and, to me, totally obscure treatise was a carefully prepared script of this bizarre "play" by this unknown "theatre." I read the piece from beginning to beginning and end to end, and found it quite wonderful but certainly difficult to perform. I was particularly struck by the blatant absence of either stage directions or common theatrical logic. Then, when I discovered that the Firesign Theatre was actually a recording group and that this "play" was in fact a phonograph recording, my job was unfounded! I immediately purchased "Dwarf" and the two other works they had produced to date for Columbia, and soon thereafter I conceived and set into motion the first pilot class of what was to become an entirely new course of studies here at school—a course in Electronic Subcultures.

As my subsequent inquiries into the Firesign phenomenon revealed, their cult of followers was small, fanatic and generally young, either in age or spirit. I found that the four members of the Firesign had performed on stage, but only in limited appearances on various college campuses on the East and West Coasts, as well as a place called The Ash Grove—a radical, funky folk club in Los Angeles. Primarily, however, they were recording artists; and, oddly enough in this day and age, radio performers!

How did this all come to be? Well, apparently frustrated in attempts over the last five years to evolve their comic improvisations and scripts on popular AM radio, they did find an outlet for such expression on radio station KPFK—a Pacifica listener-sponsored outlet in Los Angeles, where they broadcast even today and base their syndicated show. Nonetheless, they found the arena of the recorded arts to offer the most freedom of creative control without censorship, since the public is quite free to purchase records at will for private listening at home. So, working in the virgin field of virgin vinyl, Austin, Bergman, Ossman and Proctor created comedy-drama on discs, utilizing the advancing technology of the eight- and sixteen-track stereo and quadrosonic recorders under professional conditions and produced a form of entertainment that was at once amusing, puzzling and enlightening. Furthermore, in drawing upon the past and present traditions of communication—radio, records, television, theater, poetry, the novel, and the newspaper—they had evolved a new form that was greater than the sum of its parts, a form that

14   could be experienced with the imagination of the listener fully exposed.

Thus, these recorded journeys have been able to attract and influence a special audience, much as radio did in its golden era—with one major difference: It is an audience of individuals able to "listen" with incredible freedom of choice—sometimes alone, sometimes with friends, sometimes with strangers, sometimes "high," sometimes in a car, or surprised somewhere listening to a radio!

And what of the images created? And of their effect? The "stories" that the Firesign Theatre weaves exist and function on many levels—political, mythological, sociological, philosophical, and of course on the dream-like level of psychic or psychedelic symbolism. To quote Bottom in *A Midsummer Night's Dream:*

"I have had a most rare vision! I have had a dream past the wit of man to say what dream it was: —Man is but an ass if he go about to expound this dream . . . The eye of man hath not heard, the ear of man hath not seen, man's hand is not able to taste, his tongue to conceive, nor his heart to report, what my dream was . . ."

These "dreams" seem to become a part of the audience's psychic life—passed on in the culture as catch-phrases, myths and secret languages made up of jokes and puns—and so the Firesign subculture, created electrically, communicated eclectically, is born.

Indeed, our school is not the only one to presently teach classes based on the Firesign works. Many Modern American Literature courses now include the Firesign as well, as though these recordings, transcribed by loyal listeners, treated as comic books or almost as dictionaries by many—as though they were a kind of "spoken book"—an instant replay novel—a recyclable talking tome—a book for the blind in an age where the one-eared man is king!

The Firesign Theatre is avant-garde. The Firesign Theatre is Alpha-bet waves. The Firesign Theatre is almost chemical, and certainly psychedelic.

Still—as presented to us here in transcript form, I beg you, take them for what they are: scenarios toward an inner journey into the very stuff from which our dreams are made—and particularly our peculiar American daydreams and nightmares. And please, don't be confused by the pictures, they're only there to befuddle you! Just read the texts and let your mind roll on. And then, if you've never had the pleasure, buy the records, put them on, turn down the lights, close your eyes, and let the Firesign Theatre read *you*. . . .

Peter Savatte

Professor Emeritus
Solid State University
Midburn, Wisconsin

Who Am Us Anyway?

I always wanted to be a part of something. Annalee and I used to secretly, separately, dream of rock and roll bands. I hadn't even *thought* yet that rock and roll could save me.

So I was in Hollywood in 1966, starving on all levels. I got a job in a radio station because I could always do that with my voice—could make you believe that I was committed to the words coming out of my mouth. I mistakenly believed, therefore, that I was an Actor. I'm not. I'm a musician. Interesting that it was the *sounds* of the words that got to me most. The Firesign Theatre was the vehicle that allowed me to make that discovery.

The Firesign Theatre is a *Technique.*

These were the people who faced me across the microphones on the radio and this is what I think of them:

David Ossman is the first I met. The two of us are not what you'd think of right off as comedians. I was producing all these plays by dead authors—acting, directing; got David to act, looked at the amazing books of poetry that he'd produced—as if he had hand-printed every page. We had wonderful conversations about Indians. Hopi.

Peter Bergman was the Voice That Wouldn't Die. What a talker! The Champ. I engineered *Radio Free Oz* and appeared in a variety of stoned disguises. (This was fun. Not like acting, which is not real to me, therefore not fun.) Unlike most performers, Peter becomes *more* candid when he performs. Set him in front of a microphone and you have an angel. With most people, it's the opposite.

Philip Proctor *is* an actor. He is also not exactly a comedian. He is not so much trying to make you laugh as he is trying to explain something to you. I have always been his friend because I admire that so much. He can go places I can't. He was a friend of Peter's who was "funny." God, ain't dat de trufe!

So there we were, *four friends*. You see, we had no ambitions. It was a pure jam and the instrument we each played was verbal glibness or *radio*. We still continue that first conversation. This book, those recordings, are records of that conversation, a minute-book of the meeting.

Quickly, Ambition walked in the door. I thought we were good. I'd heard some pretty fast, funny cats in my time, but these three were as good as Spike Milligan. We started hanging out with each other, gave up our jobs, found more and more ways to earn livings using each other. I got my Globe Theatre, Phil P. got a Movie Company, David got a Great Work of Literature and Peter got the Forever Radio Show.

Records are Records (recordings of something). *They are meant to include you in our conversation.*

Yes, we take it seriously. Read Hideo (David) Gump Sr.'s intro to each script. Laughter and Dancing, Singing and Love. We love The Firesign

16   Theatre. How do you get along with people? What do you have to show for it? Our work is, to me, my answer to those questions.

What does it mean?

1. The Firesign Theatre writes communally. Every word goes through four heads for approval. We therefore write very slowly. Our energy level is intense. Grown men leave the room when we fight with each other. Nothing is sacred.

2. Therefore, there are considerable areas of chance (*chance*) in our work since no overall motive is possible. All communal endeavors learn one thing, I think. *Only real things can be agreed upon.* The future is not real, therefore *motives* cannot be agreed upon. *Chance becomes the motive.*

What do we mean? We mean whatever's happening. ¿Que pasó, hombre?

Our records are records of what happened to us during the period we made them.

Our records are a continuous story that will last as long as our friendship.

May we be friends forever.

Phil Austin

I was born in a trunk in The Princess Theatre, Pocatello, Idaho. No, I was born in Goshen, Indiana. I really have spent some time analyzing it. I grew up in an essentially schizophrenic existence. I was schooled on the East Coast, because I moved there when I was five. I went to Riverdale Country School and Yale University, but during my formative years of growth—the pubic years—I grew up in Goshen, Indiana, with my grandparents and my neighborhood friends. Radio and comic books had a lot to do with my youth. The comic books supplied the visual element. I finally became a professional actor after college. Acting led me to The Firesign Theatre because I found New York theater to be dumb and limited. Silly. I wanted to create my own theater.

Philip Proctor

I'm a writer, a poet, which is to say I always did that. My life was totally in my head, and I wrote about it. I developed a historical sense of things and then I went into radio. Because that's what I always wanted to do. It was one of those childhood fantasies like growing up to be a fireman. I wanted to be a radio announcer, and in 1959 I became a radio announcer. I did that for quite a while. I worked in New York at WBAI for two years and then went back to the West Coast and worked for KPFK for four years. They laid everybody off, including me, so I got a job in television, which I hated, so I dropped out of that. The Firesign Theatre appeared at the same time.

I owe everything I do to my normal childhood. I had a very unrepressed childhood and I lived in the Midwest, and there were very few things to amuse myself, except softball, so I would do routines to myself, like "Why Isn't Everybody Happy?" was one of my routines, so they kept me indoors a lot. A kid named Bruce Berger and I opened up a parking lot one night in an empty lot across from an Emporium show. We made $50 wearing Cleveland Indians baseball caps, yelling, *"Park and Lock It! Not Responsible!"*

My honest idea of The Firesign Theatre is four artists getting together and grouping to create some new art form, some multi-art that comes out of all four of their minds. It's an interesting choice, and that's one of the things that fascinates me. It's not a loss of identity, really. It's more a gaining of a double identity. I'm Peter Bergman and I'm one-quarter of The Firesign Theatre. And when I have those two things together, in harmony, one feeds off the other.

THE FIRESIGN THEATRE

ELECTRICIANS
IN LOBBY

SMITH & BATTISTE
ELECTRIC

WAITING FOR THE ELECTRICIAN
OR SOMEONE LIKE HIM

Revolution or Revelation?

" Revolution is revelation, and is turning, turning into new things, turning into new ideas, turning around to look behind you, turning and observing what's happening . . . and becoming part of the flow, translating it into your life. The reason most people become afraid and paranoid is because they are afraid to understand where they *are*, what they exist in . . . and that they are a part of it, they have made it, just as much as any machine has made it. We must wrest the control away from these short-sighted people and become involved again in an action of Being, of present time, and, more importantly, in asserting our humanity in whatever we do. Most people are incapable of this because they live in closed systems and they have been taught, brainwashed, into believing that this is the only way to exist, whereas everything else is changing, no matter what the system says. " *Philip Proctor*

" I don't dig Revolution. It's a wheel. First Julius Hoffman on top, then Abbie Hoffman . . . Julius, Abbie . . . " *Peter Bergman*

May I See Your Passport Please?

When we began the first album, the first thing we agreed to write about was the American Indian. It was not only the natural ground, the Ur-fact about life on the North American continent, but we had been tremendously impressed by the Hopi Prophesy and moved by a way-of-life which had long been maintained as a pure alternative to the one in which we found ourselves. So we wrote a history of the Indian and called it "Temporarily Humboldt County."

History lesson concluded, we found ourselves (as always) in the Present. It was Los Angeles and 1967, the Year Of The Love-In. Marijuana was in every brownie, acid in every cup of punch and Sgt. Pepper on every turntable. What was happening? Was it Chocolate, Strawberry or W.C. Fields Forever?

Only the Future would tell. It was obvious that we were living through the beginnings of a Revolution, during which even the names of the months might be changed, as in 18th Century France. So we projected ourselves as far as we could—all the way to the literary end of our "War in Nigeria," on the 38th day of Cunegonde.

Thus, America's Past, our Present, and that vision of the Present which we call "Future." When we had written these three short pieces, we turned to a longer work, something we knew we were going to call "Waiting For The Electrician or Someone Like Him" even before we realized that it's subject matter was Power. Because things already seemed to be well underway, we began on Side Five with a language lesson and a character called "P" (because Phil played the part, and in homage to Kafka's Josef K.).

So it is that "P" finds himself getting off an airplane (the Enola McLuhan?) in the dangerously neutral country of "Enroute," from which escape seems impossible. His identity is put in question, he is deliberately isolated and harassed. He cannot understand the language or where he is being sent. He arrives late, of course, to a gathering in the honor of a dying War Hero. He escapes the revolutionary holocaust which follows, receives instruction in Command and, from his underground post in the Generator Room (as close to The Grid as one can safely get), he takes over.

No sooner has he done so, but he is thrown into prison, where his aged alter-ego and a host of faceless prisoners try to make him see the hopelessness (and stupidity) of his position. Faced with an electrical death sentence, "P" reverts to childhood and wakes from his nightmare on the stage of a TV quiz show. He has been here before, too! Back now, once again, to try and find out what it is that's killing him. It's The Plague! Everybody wants it! It's what's happening! "P" makes a final desperate dash for safety, and is picked up by a friendly cabdriver—a driver who seems to be an agent for another unnamed Power.

"P," on orders from the driver, shucks off his clothes—his contagion—and throws them to the ravening crowd. The cab smashes through the border crossing, and just as the whole cycle begins again (for beyond every border lies another country Enroute) someone who knows how pulls the plug. The cycle is broken.

WAITING FOR THE ELECTRICIAN OR SOMEONE LIKE HIM

ANNOUNCER: This is Side Five. Follow in your book and repeat after me as we learn three new words in Turkish: Towel . . . Bath . . . Border . . . May I see your passport, please?

SOUND: *The background of a large terminal.*

P: Yes, I have it right here.

GUARD 1: Hmmmm. [*Ripping out a page*] Look at this.

GUARD 2: Hmmmm. This photograph doesn't look a bit like you now, does it, sir?

P: Well, it's an old picture.

GUARD 2: Precisely!

P: Is there anything wrong?

GUARD 1: Oh, no, no, no, no! Would you mind waiting over there, sir? Oh, just leave your bags.

P: But, my passport . . .

GUARD 1: Next, please!

INFORMATION MAN: Information! May I help you, sir?

P: Yes, I'd like to know . . .

INFORMATION MAN: Not for twelve hours! You'll be informed at your hotel.

P: Yes, but . . .

INFORMATION MAN: Would you like to send a wire?

P: Yes, I guess I better.

INFORMATION MAN: One moment, please.

WIREMAN: All right, sir! Do you want this to be a night letter, regular, or guaranteed delivery?

P: Which is fastest?

WIREMAN: Hah! At this time of day they all receive equal attention, depending of course on the Zone involved. Which Zone was that, sir?

P: I'm sending it overseas.

WIREMAN: No, please! The Zone! Look at the map!

P: Oh. Oh, well, then I suppose it would be . . .

GUARD 1: I beg your pardon, sir, but is this your bar of soap?

P: Well, I suppose it is.

GUARD 1: So do we.

WIREMAN: All right, sir, your telegram has been sent. You'll be receiving it in about an hour, Guaranteed Delivery. That will be two hundred and seventy-five, sir. No tax.

P: Well, I haven't had a chance to change my money yet.

GUARD 1: Just a moment, sir. Is this your bag?

P: No, it's not.

GUARD 1: Check it again. Do take your time, sir.

P: This is definitely not my bag!

GUARD 1: Just as we thought. Sign here, please. And here . . . and here . . and here . . . and here . . . and here . . . and here. Thank you, sir.

GUARD 2: We've sent your bags on ahead, sir. Where is it that you're staying?

P: Ah . . . what's the best hotel in town?

INFORMATION MAN: Of course! [*calls*] Taxi! [*then, apologetically*] Oh, ha, ha! The taxis, they are all on strike, and it's too early for the bus. You really are a problem, sir. I suppose we'll have to put you up.

ELEVATOR BOY: Going Up!

SOUND: *Elevator door closes. Sound of elevator and passing floors.*

FELLOW RIDERS: *Skajítyeh, továrish! Kak vwee padoómityeh a náshyeh górodyeh?* . . . Oh, excuse me, but my friend would like to know how much you have enjoyed our City so far?

P: Actually, I haven't been here too long.

FELLOW RIDERS: *Il n'est pas passé beaucoup de temps ici.* . . . *Noo! Rasskaziváyetsah meenyáh "dah" eélee "nyet"!* . . . Oh! He want to know "yes" or "no."

P: Well, tell him "yes." [*Raising his voice*] It's a beautiful City!

FELLOW RIDERS: *Nyeh Kricháyehtyeh! Yah slíshayoo!* . . . He says, "He can shout, don't hear you." . . . Have you seen the Palace?

P: Not yet, but I certainly intend to.

FELLOW RIDERS: Oh, you must, you must! It won't be here much longer, you know. They are cleaning it! . . . *On yedeénstvehnee?* . . . Are you alone?

P: Yes.

FELLOW RIDER: No! We are here with you.

P: Oh, I see what you mean. Uh . . . no.

FELLOW RIDER: Yes . . . How many are we?

P: Here? Three?

FELLOW RIDER: You don't want to count the elevator boy?

P: Uh, yes.

FELLOW RIDER: Three or four?

P: Four.

FELLOW RIDER: But, of course, there's your family.

P: But they're not traveling with me.

FELLOW RIDER: Where?

P: Where I'm going.

FELLOW RIDER: But you're here! How many?

P: Four. With the elevator boy.

FELLOW RIDER: Ah! He is in your family!

P: No, here!

FELLOW RIDER: And here we are . . .

SOUND: *Tinkly piano music and background crowd.*

FIELD MARSHAL: Ladies and gentlemen, our Distinguished Guest has just arrived. [*To* P] Here, have some champagne.

A GUEST: What kept you so long?

P: What do you mean?

FIELD MARSHAL: Here, come this way.

GENERAL: Gentlemen! Port and cigars in the War Room. Lord Kitchener will join us presently.

FIELD MARSHAL: Hurry along, now.

A GUEST: You've kept us waiting so long.

P: Oh, I'm sorry, I didn't realize . . .

GENERAL: Gentlemen, gentlemen, please! In these troubled times, besieged as we are on all fronts . . .

MAN IN THE CROWD: Here! Here!

GENERAL: . . . There is but one man in whom we can place with complete assurance our Faith, Hope and Destiny . . .

ANOTHER MAN IN CROWD: There! There!

GENERAL: A man who has won more battles than he has fought!

YET ANOTHER MAN: Where? Where?

GENERAL: A man who has the confidence of his people! Our generated, veneered leader! Our own Fighting Jack! Lord Kerchner . . . er . . . Kitchener!

SOUND: *Applause from the crowd. Lord Kitchener clears his throat before beginning his speech, but this turns into a cough, which he tries to assuage by drinking a glass of water, but the fit continues and the pitcher drops out of his hand and crashes to the floor.*

P: He knocked over the pitcher!

SOUND: *Kitchener's coughing fit gets worse and worse, until finally he gags and falls over on the platform. There is a short silence, broken by light, then steadily growing applause.*

P: He's . . . he's dead!

ACHMET: You'd better come with us.

P: I . . . I can't . . .

ACHMET: We are no longer safe here. Let's to the Winter Palace, quickly!

SOUND: *A door opening into a large hall.*

P: Oh! It's the Ice Show!

SOUND: *Orchestral fanfare.*

RINGLEADER: Und yetz, from der Berliner Ice Palace und Festspiel, der fun-

THESE PREMISES UNDER
CONSTANT PHOTO SURVEILLANCE
AND PROTECTED BY TIME DELAY
LOCKS ON SAFES AND VAULTS

YONI: Hello! Hello!

HANS: Hello! Hello!

YONI: Say hello, Hans!

HANS: Hello, Hans!

YONI: No, you dumbelly!

SOUND: *Yoni hits Hans and the crowd laughs. Then Hans shoots Yoni and there is more applause. Then the bombs begin to drop and planes come with rockets and there is a lot of crying and screaming as the whole place seems to go up.*

GUY 1: Psssst! Which side are you on?

P: Side Two.

GUY 1: You're with us. Come with me.

SOUND: *A door opens and they walk down an echoing corridor.*

P: Where are you taking me?

GUY 1: We don't have much time, and there's a lot you have to know.

GUY 2: Now, listen carefully. If the Revolution is to be successful . . .

GUY 1: Excuse me. Wait . . .

GUY 2: First . . .

GUY 1: But . . . but . . .

GUY 2: But . . .

GUY 1: The Revolutionary Leadership . . .

GUY 2: No, I'm talking about the Codification.

GUY 1: Go ahead . . .

GUY 2: The Codification is the Central Control . . .

GUY 1: Wait!

GUY 2: Top Secret . . .

GUY 1: Excuse me! The Protocol . . . the Protocol . . .

GUY 2: Don't tell him about the situation yet . . .

GUY 1: Let me! Let me . . . do you mind?

GUY 2: All right, go ahead.

GUY 1: I was going to . . .

GUY 2: The expediency . . .

GUY 1: According to Regulations . . .

P: Check!

GUY 1: Right!

GUY 2: Right!

GUY 1: Everything has got to be done in this time . . .

GUY 2: We've got to have Priority of Rank!

P: Right!

GUY 2: Do you mind if I . . . ?

GUY 1: Go. Go right ahead.

P: Of course!

GUY 2: There is Absolute Security necessitated . . .

GUY 1: No . . . no . . .

P: Right!

GUY 2: In all of these Operations . . .

GUY 1: But . . . but . . .

P: I'll take it from here! Follow me!

BOTH GUYS: Right, Chief!

SOUND: *Doors close behind them. Many busy voices are "Checking" and rechecking.*

P: Gentlemen, gentlemen! I won't take any more credit for this Victory than is necessary. Lord Kitchener did not—nay, will not—die in vain, Grid Willing. [*Over applause*] Gentlemen, gentlemen! I as Leader will use Power like a drum and Leadership like a violin. Pick out any Idea. Compare Ideas. With the One Idea left you have no Doubt, and without a Doubt we have Enthusiasm!

SOUND: *Much applause and cries of "Prego!" and "Pardon!"*

P: Gentlemen, gentlemen! Please, gentlemen! To make Life hold—it's as easy as a Bridge! Now, now, gentlemen! Gentlemen, now that we have attained Control we must pull together as One! Like a Twin! Keeping the Prophesy of Power as Enthusiasm! All for one!

CROWD: All for one!

P: And all for one!

CROWD: And all for one!

P: Let me hear it for me!

CROWD: You're under arrest!

SOUND: *Metal door clangs shut.*

OLD JIM: 'Ello! My, it will be pleasant to 'ave you 'ere! I've not had any company in this dank and dismal cell for forty long and miserable years. [*Reading*] I was imprisoned by a faceless people for a crime of which I had no knowledge and certainly did not commit. But what of that? In me spare time, I have been pursuing me 'obby, which is writin' a Great Prison Novel. In the beginning, I wrote with an ink composed of parts of me own blood. However, this would not make an acceptable carbon, so I acquired an electric typewriter. I am proud to present you with the first edition of me saga of eternal torment (profusely illustrated) titled "Leather Thighs"!

P [*Calling*]: Guard! Guard! I want to see my Ambassador!

FRENCH PRISONER: Easily done! He's in the next cell!

SCANDINAVIAN PRISONER: Use de telephone . . .

P: I don't have a dime!

OLD JIM: Here, use one of the pages of me novel.

SOUND: *He dials the phone only to get a Fred Astaire dance routine over the wire.*

P: It's no good, they're tapping the lines! If I could only speak to someone. If I could only tell my story!

SCREW: Famous Writer to see the condemned man.

WRITER: Oh, you poor brute of a killer without a conscience! I'm wet with compassion!

OLD JIM: Excuse me, but it's always a pleasure to meet another member of the writing fraternity. Perhaps you would like to 'ear an excerpt from me Great Prison Novel of Eternal Torment—"In Cold Leather"!

P: Oh, God!

FATHER O'LONG: Aye, what's troubling you, son?

P: Padre, I'm tired of living, and . . .

SINGING PRISONER: "Old Man River . . ."

ANOTHER PRISONER: "Ribber!" "Ribber!"

SINGING PRISONER: "Ribber . . ."

FATHER O'LONG: Now, give me that gun.

P: I don't have a gun, Father.

FATHER O'LONG: Here, have one of mine!

SOUND: *A crowd of* PRISONERS *begins to jeer and yell "Chicken!"*

P: I'm not afraid of Justice! I know these bars are here for a good reason. Prisons are for the guilty!

PRISONER: String him up!

ANOTHER PRISONER: Anybody got any string?

YET ANOTHER PRISONER: He's just like The Kid!

P: No, no, no! Don't you guys see? The System is here for your protection! I'm not afraid! All I want is a chance to clear my name! Look, we live and operate under the Due Process of Law. The Innocent have nothing to fear. Only the Guilty will suffer!

PRISONER: Lynch him!

ANOTHER PRISONER: Anybody got any lynch?

YET ANOTHER PRISONER: He even looks like The Kid!

P: Look! Look! It's this simple! I'll get a hearing and a trial. I'm willing to place my Fate and Faith in the Hands of Justice!

SOUND: *An electric generator drones, rises in pitch, then suddenly falls away in a low hum.*

P: What happened to the lights?

PRISONER: They just burned The Kid!

P: Mother!! Mama!! Mama!! I'll be good, Mama! I will, Mama! I'll be good, Mama! I just want to get out!! [*Fading into echoes*]

ATTENDANT 1: Hey, man! You think he's going to make it?

ATTENDANT 2: I don' know. He looks pretty sick to me.

P: [*Groans*]

ATTENDANT 1: Hey! I think he's coming around!

ANNOUNCER: He's coming around, folks! He's going to be OK, and ready to play Symptom Six of "Beat The Reaper!"

SOUND: *Quiz Show theme music on the organ and audience applause.*

OFF-CAMERA ANNOUNCER: Last week, our Patient successfully survived the common cold, measles, pneumonia, dengué fever, and the yaws . . .

ANNOUNCER: And now, the Big Question! Are you ready to Go On?

P: Ah . . . wha . . . where?

ANNOUNCER: He's ready!

SOUND: *More organ music and applause.*

OFF-CAMERA ANNOUNCER: And now our Topless Nurse Judy is wheeling our Patient into the Isolation Ward.

ANNOUNCER: Can you hear me in there? OK, let's Shoot Him Up!

SOUND: *The Shot!*

ANNOUNCER: Now, Patient, you have ten seconds to tell us what you've got and "Beat The Reaper!"

SOUND: *Time clock begins to tick.*

P: Ah . . . I'm shaky . . . I'm feverish . . . my hands are all . . . I'm turning yellow! My God, I've got Jaundice!

ANNOUNCER: Jaundice it is! Give him the antidote, Judy!

SOUND: *Theme music and applause.*

ANNOUNCER: Well, that's Symptom Six, and now you've reached the Final Threshold! Here's the Question. Are you ready for Symptom Number Seven, longer than any Patient has ever survived before?

P: I want to go home.

ANNOUNCER: Only one way to do that! Doctor, bring in the Super Shot!

OFF-CAMERA ANNOUNCER: Now, for the first time on "Beat The Reaper!" we're going for the Big Disease. The Icebox is being unlocked by the President of the Armenian Medical Association, under whose strict supervision these toxins are being administered.

P: [*Groans*]

ANNOUNCER: This is it! Doctor, give him that Really Big Disease!

SOUND: *The Shot!*

ANNOUNCER: Now, Patient—can you hear me? You've got ten seconds to tell us what you've got and, for the last time, "Beat The Reaper!"

SOUND: *Time clock begins to tick.*

P: I feel . . . [*coughs*] . . . I think I feel . . . I don't know . . . whatever it is . . . I want to die . . .

SOUND: *The clock runs out and the penalty buzzer sounds.*

ANNOUNCER: Oh! I'm terribly sorry, that's not correct! You didn't "Beat The Reaper!" Doctor, bring the Patient out and show the amphitheater audience and all the folks at home just what he's contracted.

DR FLITH: According to my careful prosthesis, this man has The Plague.

ANNOUNCER: Thank you, Doctor.

DR FLITH: You're welcome.

ANNOUNCER: You've got The Plague. Well, isn't he a good sport, folks? We'll be back in just a moment with our next Patient, but first . . .

SOUND: *Under the organ theme, the crowd begins to murmur, "Plague! He's got the Plague!" The murmur grows into a confused shout, lost in city traffic noise.*

DRIVER: Taxi, buddy?

P: Oh, thank God!

DRIVER: Where to, Mac?

P: Out!

DRIVER [*taking off*]: Sure thing! I'll take you to the Border. I'm gonna have to cut through the Park.

P: Is that the fastest way?

DRIVER: Uh, no, it ain't, but the Plague's got the streets all tied up.

P: Well, just do the best you can.

DRIVER: Sure thing.

P: Hey! Are those my bags?

DRIVER: Oh, yeah! We've been watching you every step of the way, but we ain't had a chance to contact you 'til now!

P: You mean . . . ? You mean . . . ?

DRIVER: Sure. What do you mean?

P: Well, I mean . . .

DRIVER: Listen, buddy, let me give you a piece of advice. What you don't mean won't hurt ya. Mind if I turn on the radio?

SOUND: *Radio turned on.*

RADIO NEWSMAN: . . . in a massive traffic tie-up, as the death-rate continues to soar. Now, let's go to the river's edge, and Charles B. Smith.

SOUND: *Remote band music and fireworks.*

CHARLES B SMITH: Ed, it's an amazing scene here. Like lemmings, the crowds are waiting on the shore, torches blazing, as the long line of shrouded funeral rafts drift lazily into view, great black candles flickering at helm and stern. The excitement is contagious, and so are the Black Cross Volunteers, as they pass from family to family, pausing now and again to touch a child's head. I wish I could . . . but I can't. So long, Ed. [*Remote transmission breaks off*]

NEWSMAN: Thank you, Charles. And now, here's another feature in our continuing report on the . . .

SOUND: *Radio is clicked off.*

DRIVER: Hey, Mac! What'd you turn it off for?

P: How close are we to the Border?

34　DRIVER: Well, at this rate . . . oh, oh! I think they spotted you!

SOUND: *The crowd shouting and screaming and banging on the taxi.*

CROWD VOICES: I want to die! There he is! He's got it! Me! Me! What about me!

DRIVER: Get out of the way! Go find your own carrier!

P: Can't we go any faster?

DRIVER: There's too many of them.

P: What can we do?

DRIVER: I don't know . . . Throw 'em your coat!

CROWD VOICES: Me! Me! Throw it to me! I wanna die!

DRIVER: Here's the Border up ahead!

P: Thank God!

DRIVER: No, not yet. We'll never make it through that crowd at the gate unless you do exactly what I say. Take off all your clothes!

P: What?

DRIVER: Come on, buddy! Take 'em off!

P: All right.

DRIVER: Now, when I give the signal, toss 'em out, and I'll drive this heap right through the barrier. Ready?

P: Yes, yes, that's everything.

DRIVER: OK, here we go!

SOUND: *The car door opens. The crowd is all around, yelling "Me, me, me!"*

DRIVER: Now!

SOUND: *A great skid and a crash, echoing into emptiness. Out of the silence, someone comes running and panting.*

ANNOUNCER: Hurry. Over here. This way. That's it! You've made it. Welcome to Side Six. Follow in your book and repeat after me, as we learn our next three words in Turkish: Coffee . . . Delight . . . Border . . . May I seeeee [*slowing as the power is cut*] yooouuurrr . . . passspooorrtt . . . pleeeaaassssssee . . .

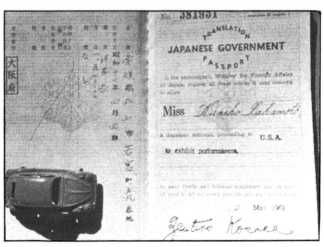

THE FIRESIGN THEATRE

How Can You Be In Two Places At Once When You're Not Anywhere At All

The Perfect Ralph Williams Mantra

Proctor: When I first came out here, I watched TV because I didn't know how to drive. I really was trapped. It was awful. So I brought my television set out, plugged it in, and I watched a lot of TV. Naturally, I saw a lot of Ralph Williams, and being stoned in front of the television or not, it didn't make any difference, I noticed it had a religious feeling to it. Once the ad came on, you turned it off mentally. So what you got was a rhythm, and numbers. So I called it the Ralph Williams Mantra. I wrote it down and performed it for the guys and that was it. And from Ralph, a lot of structuring for other kinds of Mantras came about.

Ossman: When Peter came back from Europe, I said, "Phil's got the perfect Ralph Williams Mantra, you know, and he spends a good deal of time in the bathroom because of it." Ralph became Ralph Spoilsport, one of the sponsors on "Freak For A Week," one of our radio skits. He was great, always a guaranteed laugh, and gradually all of us began to be able to do that voice.

Proctor: We had discovered the American Salesman. He got written into the "How Can You Be In Two Places At Once" side of the record, which was to be his apotheosis. The apotheosis of Ralph Williams because he talks over himself, five times. All of us do it.

Welcome To Side Six

The starting point was the Ralph Williams Mantra. Ralph live. Ralph on TV. Ralph on the AM and on the FM. Ralph in Mexico, Moscow and Paris! A dubbed Italian adventure movie running underneath the whole thing.

Then came the Car itself. It was a used 1984 Nark Avenger, but it had a Trip-Master tape cartridge that not only told you where you were and where you were going, but introduced the parts of the engine in music and song, like an "educational" children's record.

Unfortunately, the musical extravaganza so confused the car's driver that he took the wrong off-ramp and ran out of gas on an old back road. The Trip-Master abandoned him with a warning to turn on his Climate Control and wait for help.

Under the spell of a Tropical Downpour, the driver fell asleep and into a delirious dream of Traveling . . .

This was the original beginning of "How Can You Be." It was as if the character "P" had come running across The Border and had escaped, only to find himself on Ventura Boulevard in Encino. His new name is "Babe" and his odyssey continues with the act of buying a car "to get away from it all."

In the recorded version, Babe falls asleep in his car and finds himself stranded in the woods where a strange crew of "little men" (Gremlins? Dwarfs? Leprechauns?) pop up inside his head. They taunt him, and make terrible sport of him, and do W.C. Fields imitations and bad puns. The only way out of this dream seems to be through a frightening black hole that opens into . . . a tomb? a pyramid? the Great Seal of The United States?

But it turns out to be a Motel, for where else would a weary traveler go when he's been driving all day and it's been raining and he's sleepy? This Motel, however, has a couple of drunken conventioneers on hand to greet Babe, and they know who he *really* is. He's an American!

So the inspiring story of America and its people is performed for and with Babe, in a style partly borrowed from the patriotic radio and stage pageants that the WPA did so stirringly in the 1930s. But when the 1940s rolled around, so did the caissons; and so, of course, Babe's fate is to be drafted into that great equalizer of minorities, the US Army.

Or is it Babe's fate? Possibly he has drifted into another dream while watching an old movie on the car's TV—a movie called "Babes In Khaki," in which the War is Brought Back Home. But the movie is finally over, and it's Late Late. Once through the dial, where that dubbed Italian movie about Ulysses is playing again (still?) and where Ralph sponsors everything.

Time to have a little toke and drift back into sleep . . .

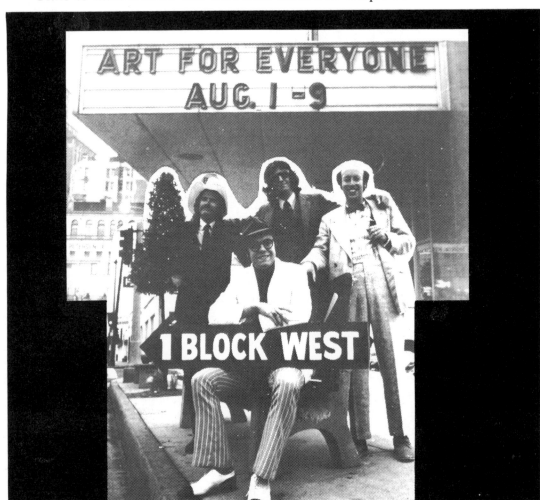

How Can You Be In Two Places At Once When You're Not Anywhere At All

SOUNDS: *Street and traffic noises under.*

RALPH: Hiya, friends! Ralph Spoilsport, Ralph Spoilsport Motors, the world's largest new used and used new automobile dealership, Ralph Spoilsport Motors, here in the City of Emphysema. Let's just look at the extras on this fabulous car! Wire-wheel spoke fenders, two-way sneezethrough windvent, star-studded mudguards, sponge-coated edible steering column, chrome fender dents, and factory air-conditioned air from our fully factory-equipped factory. It's a beautiful car, friends, with doors to match! Birch's Blacklist says this automobile was stolen, but for you, friends, the complete price, only two thousand five hundred dollars, in easy monthly payments of twenty-five dollars a week, twice a week, and never on Sundays . . .

BABE [*calling*]: Ralph! Ralph!

SOUND: *Cars screeching as Babe runs through traffic.*

BABE: I'll take it! I'll take it! I can't wait to get away from it all!

RALPH: Well, OK, fine! Let's just take a look inside your beautiful new home! Come on in!

SOUND: *A car door opens and closes, silencing the street sounds.*

BABE: Thanks . . .

RALPH: As you can see, this car's been fully equipped with a complete line of extras, designed with your mind in mind!

BABE: Wow!

RALPH: Here, for instance, an all-weather climate control in red, blue or green, with a special oxygen danger-indicator level.

BABE: Gee whiz!

RALPH: And here, of course, your own personal remote-controlled, picture-sized color TV, with matching brass knobs! Just reach above the bar and press the button right there under the handy laminated imitation masonite Wild-West gun rack with the look of real wood, for the channel of your choice!

BABE: Ralph, can I try it?

RALPH: Sure.

SOUND: *TV set turned on.*

TV RALPH [*cutting in*]: . . . on't we do it in the road, here at Ralph Spoilsport Motors, here in the City of West Gomorra? So just give us a call at 9-1-9-9 . . . [*fading under*]

RALPH: How do ya like those colors? Isn't that nice?

BABE: Nice! Can you get UHF?

RALPH: No, I don't believe in flying saucers.

TV RALPH [*continuing under*]: . . . that's TR—Tricky on your dial . . .

RALPH: I got a little blue halo around my head.

BABE: Can I—uh, can I get a little more orange in his face?

RALPH: Sure. Right there . . .

BABE: Where? Right . . .

RALPH: No. Move that.

BABE: Under the trigger here?

RALPH: Yeah, that's right.

BABE: Just a second. I've got to get the safety off. Oh, ho, ho! Look at that blue horse!

SOUND: *TV soundtrack cuts to a movie in progress.*

MOVIE ALEXANDER: People of Alexandria! People of Alexandria! Who burned the library?

SOUND: *Crowds yelling. Movie music.*

BABE: I think I've . . . Isn't that . . . ?

RALPH: Look at the muscles on that dude! He's got muscles in his ear.

BABE: That's—uh—Steve Reeves.

RALPH: No, no.

BABE: No? Uh—there he is! That's Steve Reeves.

RALPH: No. That's Agnes Moorhead.

BABE: Oh, yeah? I thought . . . I have seen this one. Where's the bathroom?

SOUND: *The TV movie continues under.*

RALPH: Oh! Right next to the radio, completely modulated with dual left and right stereo speakers in two compatable frequencies. Your AM . . .

SOUND: *AM radio turned on.*

AM DJ: . . . Super Box Number Time! In the fifteen hundred, on the 27–62 on the digital in just a moment!

RADIO RALPH: $249.95! $387.07! $743! $70.84! Three dollars and sixty-two cents! Seven days a week, seven days a year, five days a week, 365 days a month! . . . [*continues under*]

RALPH: By the way, we also have FM. Right here.

BABE: FM over here? Let me try it.

SOUND: *FM radio turned on.*

FM ANNOUNCER: . . . so hop in your wife and head in any direction on the freeway of your choice, and we'll see you in a couple of hours, here at Ralph Spoilsport Motors, the World's Biggest, here in the City of Fine Music. Thanks for the insurrection, and now back to our morning concert of afternoon showtime favorites—the Magic Bowl movement from Symphony in C Minus by Johann Amadeus Matetsky.

SOUND: *Music on the FM.*

BABE: Hey, Ralph! That's great fidelity on that FM! Nice tone!

RALPH: You haven't heard nothing yet. I've got right here in this car, for your trans-Atlantic driving pleasure, this fully hallicrafted Sea-Master short-wave radio in this non-returnable, non-disposable zinc-lined carrying case!

BABE: Can I get Duluth on it?

RALPH: Duluth, bucko! You can get Tierra Del Fuego!

SOUND: *Short-wave radio turned on.*

LATIN ANNOUNCER: ¡Hola, amigos Latinos! Aqui a Ralph's Used Motors, tres-cientos Nort' Hoover, a la esquina de 42nd Place, tenemos milliones de automoviles . . . *[fading under]*

RALPH: Yeah, yeah . . .

BABE: Nice picture. I like it.

RALPH: What?

BABE: I like it. I like the car!

RALPH: Wait a minute! Let me just turn off some of this—we'll get back to business . . . Turn this FM off . . .

SOUND: *Radio turned off. Classical music out.*

RALPH: . . . this radio over here . . .

SOUND: *Other radios turned off.*

RALPH: OK. There . . .

BABE: I'll get the TV . . .

MOVIE OSIRUS: . . . Odysseus! Odysseus!

MOVIE ODYSSEUS: Osirus!

RALPH: No, no. Leave it on for a minute . . .

MOVIE OSIRUS: Odysseus, my friend! What has happened to your nose?

RALPH: Yeah, yeah. I have seen this before. Go ahead. Turn it off.

MOVIE ODYSSEUS: What news of my family?

MOVIE OSIRUS: Oh! Horrible, horrible!!

MOVIE ODYSSEUS: What! How did . . .

SOUND: *The TV set is turned off.*

RALPH: Well, that's it! Here's your keys. Goodbye, friends, and happy motoring back on the Freeway, which is already in progress . . . !

SOUND: *Car door opens and closes.*

BABE: Whew! Well, here goes . . .

SOUND: *Babe starts the car and begins to drive. Car sound under.*

BABE: Nice feel. Let's see . . . *[sings to himself]* "Oh, how can you be in two places at once when you're not anywhere at a-a-all!" . . . I think I'll give this old baby a spin on the Freeway . . .

ROADSIGNS: "Wrong Way" . . . "Entering Freeway" . . .

BABE: Here we go!

ROADSIGNS: "Emergency Parking Only" . . . "Merging Busses Ahead" . . .

BILLBOARD 1: "Giant Slide! 19 Holes! Underground Parking! Midden Hills Retirement Paradise! Swingers Only!"

BABE: Oh, too bad.

BILLBOARD 2: "Easy access! . . ."

ROADSIGNS: "Goldoni Avenue Half Mile" . . . "Speedometer Check—Zero" . . . "Strassburg Lane One Mile" . . .

BABE: Speedometer's only got half-a-mile on it!

ROADSIGN: "Antelope Fwy—5-in-a-shield—N Alt.—Two mi . . ."

BABE: Antelope Freeway North. Do I wanna go north, or do I wanna take the—let's see—the Gomorra Expressway West?

BILLBOARD 1: "Shadow Valley Condoms! If you lived here, you'd be home by now!"

BILLBOARD 2: "Antelope Hills. Selected Living. Comfortable. Easy. OK . . ."

ROADSIGNS: "Antelope Freeway. This Lane. Exit Only . . ."

BABE: Yeah, I think I'll take the old Antelope. Less traffic.

SIGN: "Easy Street Overpass . . ."

ROADSIGN: "Antelope Freeway One Mile . . ."

BILLBOARD 2: "Clean Up Armenia! Get a Hairlip!"

ROADSIGN: "Antelope Freeway One-Half Mile . . ."

SIGN: "Chili Avenue Overpass . . ."

BABE: Let's see what they've got in this car.

ROADSIGN: "Antelope Freeway One-Quarter Mile . . ."

BABE: Let's see . . .

ROADSIGN: "Antelope Freeway One-Eighth Mi . . ."

BABE: We've got lights, wipers, defrost . . .

ROADSIGN: "Antelope Freeway One-Sixteenth Mi . . ."

BABE: . . . temperature and Climate Control! Hummmm . . .

ROADSIGN: "Antelope Freeway One-Thirty-Second Mi . . ."

BABE: Let's see what kind of climate I can get . . .

ROADSIGN: "Antelope Freeway One-Sixty-Fourth Mi . . ."

BABE: Winter Wonderland. Spring Fever . . .

ROADSIGN: "Antelope Freeway One-One Hundred and Twenty-Eighth Mi . . ."

BABE: . . . Indian Summer . . .

ROADSIGN: "Antelope Freeway One-Two Hundred and Fifty-Sixth Mi . . ."

BABE: . . . Tropical Paradise. Tropical Paradise? I think I'll give it a try . . .

ROADSIGN: "Antelope Freeway One-Five Hundred and . . ."

SOUND: *A click. The road sounds disappear, replaced by birds, wind, crickets and frogs.*

BABE: Wow! What a groove! A Tropical Paradise!

SOUND: *Clap of thunder. Rain begins to fall. Babe yawns as the rain continues. Ducks quack and distant thunder rolls. Babe yawns and then falls silent. As the rain dwindles off, there are the sounds of footsteps sloshing through mud.*

OLD MAN [*fading in*]: Alright! This way! This way now! What a wonderful clearing in the jungle! Just the place to build our camp! Alright, you men get cracking now. The pup-tents right over there, I think. Right!

SOUND: *Dog barking. Men moving about in the wet.*

OLD MAN: The foundation should go right about here . . . The stockade! The stockade! . . .

DR DOG: Excuse me, Sir. Can I speak to you alone, Sir?

OLD MAN: Why of course you can.

DR DOG: Daddy, I've lost the Lincoln Logs!

PABLO: That's alright! I've got an Erector Set!

DR DOG: Show-off!

OLD MAN: Throw a towel over it!

DR DOG: Do some push-ups, Pablo! It'll go away! [*They all laugh uproariously*]

BABE [*startled awake*]: Hey! What are you guys doing in my car?

OLD MAN: The foxtrot! You can have the next dance. Herbert! Throw him the fox.

SOUND: *The fox being thrown.*

BABE: This animal is sick!

OLD MAN: Yes, it is a catchy little number!

BABE: [*Coughs*]

DR DOG: Oh, oh! I think he's caught it! Doctor, give him something for his cough!

DOCTOR: Alright, alright! Here's a quarter.

OLD MAN: That's not much.

DOCTOR: It's not much of a cough!

BABE: I need a gas station! Did I pass one?

OLD MAN: No, but the fox did! Squeeze him right there, maybe he'll pass another one!

BABE: No! No! Gasoline!

DR DOG: Oh, my boy, if it's drugs you want, the Old Doctor can help you out!

DOCTOR: Right this way . . .

BABE: Get your hands off me! I don't want to leave!

DOCTOR: Then roll up your arm and bend over! Do you want Regular or Premium?

BABE: Oh, this is ridiculous! You guys are nothing but a pack of cards!

ALL: Drink me! Eat me! Smoke me! . . .

OLD MAN [*singing*]: "Drink to me only with thine fox . . ."

BABE: There must be some way out of this. I'll change the air, that's what I'll do. What have I got left on the Climate Control? Dust Storm? Tibetan Wilderness? Land of the Pharaohs? Land of the Pharaohs! That sounds great! . . .

SOUND: *A click. The atmosphere is replaced by blowing sand and Arabian music.*

OLD MAN: Alright! Alright! Here we are in the Land of the Pharaohs!

BABE: Oh, no!

OLD MAN: Well, we'll need to talk to the natives. Does anyone here know a little Egyptian?

DR DOG: Bill! Bill, come on! You're good at languages!

BILL: Ah, yes! Yes, indeed . . .

DR DOG: "Yes, indeed!" The voice isn't right!

BILL [*tries again*]**:** Yes. Yes, indeed . . .

OLD MAN: That's wonderful!

BILL: Yes! A little Egyptshine? Let's see! A little Egyptsheen? Yes, everybody knows Ahmet! Served my every need. Did a grand job on my ankles, too!

BABE: Now, hold it right there!

OLD MAN: Glad to! [*Moves off*] Now, I think I'll hold it over here!

DR DOG: Oh, boy! It's nice out!

BILL: Yes. I think you ought to leave it out!

BABE: Hey! Hey, look, fellas! Fun's fun, but I've got to find a place to stay. It'll be night soon. I'm tired. I'm lost.

BILL: What's the matter with that dude?

BABE: I wanna go to bed!

BILL: Ah, my bony boy! In the Estonian Mountains, we used to go to sleep leaning up against a wind-fall. I was but a mere pratt then. I'll never forget the time a snake slithered into my wife! I wasn't but knee-high to a married grasshopper then. Never saw the woman again. . . .

BABE: No, no! That's all very interesting, but the sun is going down!

BILL: Oh, no, no! You are confused! The horizon is moving up!

BABE: Hey, listen! Come on, you guys! Help me, please!

OLD MAN: I know, I know! Let's . . .

ALL: . . . Stand him on his head!

BABE: Hey, hey! Put me down!

BILL: Easy boy!

SOUND: *They struggle with Babe.*

OLD MAN: Now, you see? Now it's morning!

BABE: Ah—ah—Help! . . .

SOUND: *He crashes down.*

DR DOG: He's no fun. He fell right over!

BABE: Oh, hey, won't somebody please help me?

BILL: Easy, easy, my lad. At times of dexterity like this, my wee native compendium Mohameet used to pray to the divinities. His little brown froggy body a-quiver at my loins, chanting a stream of ancient Egyptshine holograms . . .

BABE: What?

BILL: Eh—diaphragms? I used to date . . .

BABE: No, no! Hieroglyphs! That's it! Do you remember any? Will they help? Anything at all!

BILL: Of course! Of course, it was a jackal-headed woman with her eyes akimbo, a King sitting sideways on his throne, adrip with gold, chipped nose up-lifted—thusly! All engraven on a Pyramis of Massey size, with the body of a Lion, paws that refreshes, a tale told by an idiot, and the head of a Fox!

SOUND: *Chanting and strange music.*

BABE: That Pyramid is opening!

OLD MAN: Which one?

DR DOG: The one with the ever-widening hole in it!

BABE: I'm saved! I'm going in!

MOM [*from within the pyramid*]: No! Don't do that, son! It's dark and dirty in there!

BABE: Aw, but Mom . . .

MOM: It's full of bees and spiders! You might poke your eye out! Wait 'til your Father comes home!

BABE: I'm going in, Mom! There's a Vacancy!

SOUND: *The strange chanting builds to a climax and disappears. The "ding" of a desk-bell is heard.*

DESK CLERK: Good evening, Sir! Welcome to the only Nice Motel in town. How long will you be with us?

BABE: Just for tonight.

DC: Ah! Very well, Sir. You'll find it's very Clean here. Just fill out this card.

SOUND: *A crowd laughing and chatting in the background. Bar music.*

BABE: Oh, thanks. Oh, look—it's dirty. Somebody's already used it. There's a name on it . . .

DC: That's all right.

BABE: Well, I couldn't get you to believe my name is "Mr. and Mrs. John Smith," could I?

DC: Well, of course you could! It's Nice to have you with us, Mr. and Mrs. Smith. [*Rings bell*] Front!

EDDIE: Hey! Aren't you Mr. and Mrs. John Smith from Anytown, USA?

JOE: I'm Joe, boy, and this here's Ed.

EDDIE: Hi, fella!

BABE: I'm not really Mr. and Mrs. John Smith . . .

JOE: That's OK. I'm not Joe . . .

EDDIE: And he's not Ed! Hey, fella, how about bending a couple in the Doo-Dah Room? If you catch my meaning!

JOE: If ya get my drift!

BABE: Thanks, fellas, but I'm kinda tired. Hey, Desk Clerk—can I have my key, please?

DC: Sure! What about G7? Hit it, Jimmy!

MUSIC: *Piano under-score begins.*

JOE [*singing*]: "I can tell by the pie on your tie, . . ."

EDDIE [*singing*]: "You're an American! Well, so am I! . . ."

JOE [*singing*]: "Hi, bub! How are ya? How do ya' do? . . ."

BOTH [*singing*]: "And while we're on the subject—
    And while we're on the subject—
    (And while we're on the subject)—
    How's your Old Wazoo?"

BABE: What's that all about?

DC: What's it all about, Mr. and Mrs. John Q. Smith from Anytown, USA?

JOE: Well, it's about this long . . .

DC: And about that wide . . .

EDDIE: And it's about this country . . .

DC: About which we're singin' about!

EDDIE [*singing*]: "I was born an American!
    I was raised an American!
    And I'll die an American,
    In America, with Ar-me-ni-ans . . ."

JOE: Yes, we've got a lot of everything in this land of ours . . .

DC: And a lot of places to put it in . . .

JOE: And maybe that's where *you* fit in, Mr. and Mrs. John Q. Smith from Anytown, USA!

SOUND: *Huge crowd in an auditorium responding and singing along.*

DC: Come on, Big Fella! Take this guitar! Put on this wide belt and work-shirt and tell it like it was!

BABE: Gimme that guitar!

CROWD MAN: Hot dog!

BABE: Alright, everybody, thank you very much! A little song I learned up-stream at prison! Everybody sing along now! Ready, now . . . [*he leads the crowd in singing*]
    "This land is made of mountains!
    This land is made of mud!
    This land is made of everything
    For me and Elmer Fudd!
    This land has lots of trousers!
    This land has lots of Mausers!
    And Pussy Cats to eat them when the sun goes down!"

SOUND: *Cheering and applause.*

BABE: Thank you very much! Thank you very, very much! Thank you . . .

JOE: Stop!!

SOUND: *The auditorium crowd vanishes suddenly.*

DC: It wasn't always like that . . .

JOE: No. First they had to come from towns with strange names like . . .

EDDIE: Smegma!

DC: Spasmodic!

EDDIE: Frog!

JOE: And the far-flung Isles of Langerhans.

BABE: But who were they?

JOE & EDDIE: They were small, angry men with hairy faces and burning feet . . . We was running away from Poverty, Intolerance, the Army and the Law . . . and the Army . . .

DC: And we took to them!

EDDIE: And they took to us!

DC: And what do you think they took?

CHANTING CHORUS: Oil from Canada! Gold from Mexico! Geese from their neighbor's back yard! Boom, boom! Corn from the Indians! Tobacco from the Indians! Dakota from the Indians! New Jersey from the Indians! New Hampshire from the Indians! New England from the Indians! New Delhi from the Indians! . . .

BABE: Indonesia for the Indonesians!

SOUND: *Cannon shot.*

JOE: Yes, and Veteran's Day . . .

DC: But we couldn't do it alone!

SOUND: *Morse Code sending under.*

JOE: No! We needed the Hope, the Faith, the Prayers, the Fears . . .

DC: The Sweat, the Pain, the Boils, the Tears!

JOE: The Broken Bones!

DC: The Broken Homes!

JOE: The Total Degradation of . . .

BABE: Who?

EDDIE: You! The Little Guy!

DC: And across you-all, we flung One Shining Steel Rail! . . .

CHANTING CHORUS [*as a train*]: Rock-e-feller! Rockefeller! Humphrey! Nixon! Kennedy!

DC: From sea to mighty sea! From coast to mighty coast! From Bangor all the way to mighty Maine!

CHANTING CHORUS [*slowing and stopping*]: Wallace-s-s-ss- . . . Ford! Ford!

DC: So how about that, Mr. Smarty-Pants Communist?

SOUND: *Bronx cheers as responses to questions.*

DC: Mr. College Professor? Mr. Beatnick? Mr. Hippie? What have you done for *me* lately?

BABE: Well, I . . .

JOE: Mr. and Mrs. Smith! Go to the People! Ask the hands that serve the machines of America! Ask those thousands of folks who wouldn't say "no" to yesterday, and "yes" instead of knowing it all!

EDDIE [*singing*]: "Ask the Postman! Ask the Mailman!
       Ask the Milkman, white with foam . . . !"

CROWD MAN: Go home, scab!

JOE: Ask the cop on the corner . . .

DC: Ask the cop in the grocery store . . .

JOE: Ask the cop in the woodpile . . .

DC: Ask the cop on the rooftop . . .

JOE: Ask that cop that's knockin' at your back door . . .

SOUND: *Knocking.*

DC: Ask him!

BABE: Mr. Policeman? What makes America great?

JOE & EDDIE [*singing*]:
       "It's candied apples and ponies with dapples,
       You can ride all day.
       It's girls with pimples and cripples with dimples
       That just won't go away!
       It's spicks and wops and niggers and kikes
       With noses as long as your arm!
       It's micks and chinks and gooks and geeks
       And honkies (Honk! Honk!) who never left the farm . . ."

DC: That's America, buddy! Just remember—Abraham Lincoln didn't die in vain, he died in Washington, D. C.!

BABE: I see . . . well, who am us, anyway?

EDDIE: We're one of you, and you're one of us, I think.

JOE: Maybe . . .

DC: Possibly . . .

BABE: How do you tell? How do you know for sure? How do you ever really know?

JOE: They didn't ask questions like that back in 1776! No, they didn't have time back in 1776! Back in 1776, boy, they were too busy singing songs like . . .

EDDIE [*singing*]: "Yankee Doodle came to terms,
       Writing Martin Buber.
       Stuck a Führer in our back,
       And called it Shicklegruber!"

SOUND: *A trumpet plays Retreat.*

DC: Come on, Mr. and Mrs. Too-Busy-To-Be-A-Homecoming-Queen! Get in step with the voices of the feet already dead in the service of their Country!

SOUND: *A Dixieland Band plays.*

JOE: 1829! In the midst of an ever-deepening sense of Prosperity, Chester Allen Arthur climbed to the top of his bedroom wall, thrust his defiance at the Javanese, and shouted . . .

ARTHUR [*badly recorded*]: Give me Them, or I'm going Over There!

SOUND: *Military march music.*

DC: But in 1934, in Germany, the Specter of Doom was rising its shrouded head in agony . . .

SCHNIFTER [*in auditorium*]: Das ist immer alles Aulung und ist rauch mit and potzen Volkswagen und nieman stint und "Swell Pizza!!"

CROWD [*chants*]: Sig Freud! Sig Freud! Sig Freud! [*Fading*]

BABE: Gee, Grandpa!

DC: And did you come to her defense in those dark days then, Lad? Well, they did! They came from the endless plains of Io-way, the Lonesome Trains of Illinois and the White Trash Mountains of Virginnie . . .

EDDIE [*singing*]: "You gotta jump down, spin around! (Huhn!)
　　　　　 And pick a bale o' Dacron!
　　　　　 You gotta jump down, spin around!
　　　　　 And pick some Nylon, too!"
　　　　　 [*whipcrack*] Agggh . . .!

JOE: Yes, Them too! A lot of Them. Mostly Them and not many of Us! And that's why we're here and they're there! So there, Mr. Monday Morning Quarterback, Mr. Wheelchair General! Are you going to turn your back on America's fighting mens when he come knock, knock, knockin' at your front door?

BABE: No!

DC: Atta boy! Can't you see it all now? As if it were almost Tomorrow? Thousands of 'em!

BABE: Shoulder to shoulder!

DC: That's right!

BABE: Heart to heart!

EDDIE: You said it, kid!

BABE: Satchel to Paige!

JOE: You got it!

SOUND: *Knock on door.*

DC: You get it . . .

SOUND: *Door opening.*

RECRUITING SGT: Greetings from the President of the United States! Well? Feets git moobin'!

BABE: Yes, Sir.

SGT: What's that?

BABE: Ya-a-s Sir!

SGT: What do you say?

BABE: Ya-a-a-s Suh!!

SGT: Spreek Engrish, Troop!!

BABE: Y-a-a-a-s-s Suh!!!

SQUAD [*chanting*]: You ain't got no friends on the Left!

BABE: You're right!

SQUAD: You ain't got no friends on the Right!

BABE: You're left!

SQUAD: Hound Dog!

BABE: One! Two!

SQUAD: Poon Tang!

BABE: Tree Frog!

SQUAD: Hound Dog! Poon Tang! Coon Town!

BABE: I's White! I'd rather be White than right . . . [*fading*]

SOUND: *Distant piano music, airplanes, shelling.*

MORRIE [*off*]: I'll see what I can do, Sgt. [*coming on*] Lurlene? Honey . . . ?

LURLENE: Morrie, please don't come in now. I . . .

MORRIE: Why've ya got the lights out in here, baby? I gotta talk to you!

LURLENE: Morrie . . .

MORRIE: Honey, look—this is serious! You've got to go out there and give
   yourself to those men!

LURLENE: I can't face those boys. Not now. Not yet . . .

MORRIE: Tomorrow ain't comin' for a lot of those boys, Lurlene.

LURLENE: But, Morrie, they're all wearing Bill's face! [*Sobs*]

MORRIE: Honey, we've all got our . . . will ya please put that stuff down,
   please! What would Bill think? Excuse me—look, honey, if it wasn't for
   those millions of Boogies out there, the President of these United States
   would be named Shicklegruber! Baby, excuse me for saying it, but ever
   since Anzio you've been acting like a spoiled . . .

SOUND: *Knocking at door.*

MORRIE: I'll get it.

SOUND: *Door opens.*

BABE: Telegram fo' you, Miss DiAngelo! . . . Oh, uh—I'm sorry—I didn't
   know . . . This is for you, Ma'm . . .

LURLENE: Thank you, son. Just a minute, boy! Come here . . .

BABE: Yes?

LURLENE: Where are you from?

BABE: Nairobi, Ma'm. Isn't everybody?

LURLENE: This is for you. [*Kisses him*]

BABE: Why! Thank you, Ma'm! I just want you to know, all the boys—we be waitin' fo' you out there! God bless ya', Miss Lu'lene! [*Exits*]

MORRIE: Lemme see that telegram, will ya? Honey, that's from Washington, D.C.!

LURLENE: Oh, Morrie, I . . . my mascara is running. Will you read it for me . . . ?

MORRIE: All right. Sit down, Lurlene, this may be rough. . . . The president of the United States *is* named Schicklegruber!

LURLENE: I'm going out there, Morrie! Help me into this parachute!

MORRIE: No, no, honey! You can't go out there! It's too late!

LURLENE: Zip me up! It's never too late, Morrie! I'm going out there, because I'm Bringing The War Back Home!

SOUND: *Cuts to a giant amphitheatre, crowd stamping and cheering.*

MC: Awright, boys! Awright! Quiet down now! Here she is, that lovely piece of cake we've all been waiting for, Miss Lillie LaMont!

LURLENE [*singing*]: "We're bringing the war back home,
 Where it ought to have been before!
 We'll kill all the bees and spiders and flies,
 And we won't play in iceboxes lying on their sides!

 We'll wash our hands after wee-wee,
 And if we're a girl, before!
 And we'll march, march, march, et cetera!
 'Til we never do march no more!

 (All together now, boys!)
 We're bringing the war back home,
 Where it ought to have been before!
 The pretty donut girl on the corner
 Will be smilin' with a wringer in her hair!

 We'll wash our hands after wee-wee,
 And if we're a girl, before!
 And we'll march, march, march, et cetera!
 'Till we don't have to march no more!

 (Hum along now . . .)

SOUND: *Crowd humming under.*

NARRATOR: We'd like to express our appreciation to the United States Marines, The British Commonwealth Occupation Forces, the French Legumes, and the Hong Kong Fireworks Company, without whom all of this would not have been necessary!

LURLENE [*singing*]: "We won't have to March!
 We won't have to March!
 We won't have to March no more!"

SOUND: *Movie finale music, followed by TV signature theme.*

ANNOUNCER: You've been watching "Babes in Khaki" on the Late Late Show

for a Saturday night. Stay tuned for the Early Bird Theatre, when
George Matetsky meets Danger in the form of a beautiful woman in
"Luck . . ."

SOUND: *The* Click! *of TV changing channels, followed by white noise, another* Click! *and organ music.*

PREACHER: . . . nointed with oil on troubled waters? Oh, Heavenly Grid, help
us bear up thy Standard, our Chevron flashing bright across the Gulf of
Compromise, standing Humble on the Rich Field of Mobile American
Thinking? Here in this Shell we call Life . . .

SOUND: Click!

SPORTSCASTER: . . . Angels 3, Devils . . .

SOUND: Click! *White noise. Another* Click!

MOVIE OSIRUS: Odysseus! Odysseus!

MOVIE ODYSSEUS: My friend!

MOVIE OSIRUS: What has happened to your nos . . .

SOUND: Click! *White noise. Another* Click!

GUEST: . . . well, you got people jumping out of 'em, and you got water drop-
ping out of 'em—you really are—you know—using your heli . . .

SOUND: Click! *White noise. Another* Click!

SWINE: . . . OK, Swami, or whatever your name is, we'll be back with this
Christ Consciousness racket in just a minute.

SWAMI: No, no, Mr. Swine. It's Krishna Consciousness. You see, to our
peop . . .

SOUND: Click! *White noise. Another* Click! *Movie background of car driving on busy
street.*

NICK: . . . hate cops, Guido! I'll always hate cops!

GUIDO: Yeah, Nick! I hate cops too!

PAOLO: Yeah! Me too!

NICK: I'll tell you guys what I'm gonna do! I'll tell ya' what! I'm gonna get
even with every rotten cop in this city!

PAOLO: Yeah! Me too!

GUIDO: How ya gonna do it, Nick? How ya gonna do it?

NICK: You know what I'm gonna do?

GUIDO: No, no, Nick! Whatcha gonna do?

NICK: I'm gonna turn in my badge!

GUIDO: Yeah, yeah!

PAOLO: Yeah! Yeah!

GUIDO: Yeah! I'm gonna burn my uniform! . . .

SOUND: *Cuts to commercial background.*

RALPH: Hiya, friends! Ralph Spoilsport, owner and operator of the world's biggest dealership west of Baalbeck. As you know, we're overdosed again
with all tastes and kilos. Let's just take a look at some of these fabulous

lids! The LaGuardia Report says this key should be copped for ten thousand, five hundred dollars, in easy monthly sentences of a year-to-life, and nobody down. Our complete price to you, including sticks and stems and seeds, wine-soaked and sugar-cured, completely clean for your smoking pleasure, the complete price—only what the traffic will allow, in unmarked bills, delivered to me, Ralph Icebag, in a plain brown wrapper, by a brown-shoed square in the dead of night! Let's take a taste of this fabulous Yucatan Blue, scored to you from the sky-blue waters of that beautiful Mexican bay, hand-picked by naked little froggy native boys in their tight leather aprons, running through the fields by the sea and the sea crimson sometimes like fire and the glorious sunsets and the fig trees in the Alameda gardens yes yes and all the queer little streets and pink and blue and yellow houses and the rose gardens and the jessamine and geraniums and cactuses and Gibraltar as a boy where I was a flower of the mountains yes where I put the rose in my hair like the Andalusian girls used yes and how she kissed me under the Moorish wall and I thought well as well him as another and she asked me would I to say yes my mountain flower and first I put my arms around him yes and drew her down to me so I could feel her breasts all perfumed yes and his heart was going like mad and yes I said yes I will yes . . . yes . . . yes . . . yes . . . [*fading*] Yes-s-s-s . . .

THE FIRESIGN THEATRE

don't crush that dwarf, hand me the pliers

'The latest album is about Multiple-Identity—going through changes here and now. We are dealing with television: What the TV set gives you is the ability to plug in at any time. You can get any old movie, something from every bit of time . . . it's a life in the day of a man who looks at himself on television, metaphorically speaking . . . you can see yourself on TV, anyone of those people can be you . . . we make records of our time. We made this one at the time of the Kent State murders, so naturally we wrote about schools . . . " *David Ossman*

' This record, I think—as I am projecting now—is gonna end up in Paradise. At this point the guy, the character, is going to get out, is going to get free; because so far we haven't gotten him free. I mean, he was stoned at the end of the second record. The next one we're going to get out, we're going to do birds and trees, flowers and ducks, a lot of nice, pretty things. " *Phil Austin*

"A Life In The Day"

In January, 1968, we wrote the last script in a series of half-hour plays which we were performing on AM radio. It departed from the more absurd character-comedies we had been doing, being based on a day's television programming. Beginning with the morning's first show, "Today's Day Today," it continued (with commercial interruptions) with the day's broadcasts of "Sailor Bill," "The End of the World," "Ozzie Knows Father," The Evening News (including an item about a man-made baby), "The Golden Hind," and a Western called "Garbanza!" Late in the evening, the TV channels were changed, switching through several bits of programs, including an Italian movie and the Ralph Spoilsport-sponsored Late Late Show, "Babes In Khaki." At last, after a prayer and the National Anthem, the station and the set were turned off for the day.

The concept of channel-switching stuck and, for "How Can You Be," we incorporated this idea, expanding on several of the original scenes, and, in effect, making the Late Late Show the frame for the entire opus.

After the release of "How Can You Be," in 1969, we were scheduled to appear during Christmas week at the Ash Grove in Hollywood. For the date, we resurrected the radio script ("A Life In The Day," it was called), expanding on everything we hadn't used on record, clicking through many more channels, and ending with the ever-popular Ralph Spoilsport Mantra. This is the piece we performed while on tour in the East in March, 1970.

As the performances went on, "The TV Set" began to change. Someone would contribute a new character, commercial or TV show from night to night. The new bits were pieced into the script, which got longer and longer. Somewhere along the line, Phil Austin brought in a teenage horror movie starring some well-known comic-book figures, and Peter introduced Mrs. Presky.

60

The new record was much on our minds during the Eastern Tour. It had been decided that David would carry on the story of "P" and Babe, but the context remained hidden until we sat down at the round table after our return and started writing. It seemed sensible to begin by turning on the electricity, and, in order to let everyone know that it was "going to be all right," our old friend Pastor Flash was summoned up from The Powerhouse Church.

The Pastor arrives in his mock B-29 (the Enola McLuhan?) to the rousing strains of "Marching to Shibboleth," a song we had written to be sung in a movie called "Zachariah," which, perhaps luckily, was never made.

By the time Pastor Flash lands, he is on all-night television.

If it was Babe who fell asleep watching Ralph, it is George Tirebiter who awakes at 4 AM, ravenously hungry. The TV drones on. The advertised food is unavailable in George's area. The Pizza Man is not there. But the Pastor offers his TV flock sustenance, material as well as spiritual. And George falls for it, grabbing the glowing color-TV groat cakes right out of the tube and gorging himself on them.

The ingestion of this "food" works its changes on George, who suddenly becomes a character *on* the TV, moving through the TV world in several different guises. He is, by turns, an old movie director, a political candidate, a child star, a high-school kid, an adult actor, an Army Officer, a quiz-show MC. As George goes through his changes, the night world of the TV continues.

Someone (George himself?) switches through the channels, torn between watching "High School Madness!" and/or "Parallel Hell!" It is the black-and-white movie-world of the 1950s where Authority Questioned is, or ought to be, Authority Triumphant. And inside of it, George is on trial because he (like the JDs, Pico and Alvarado) ultimately refuses to believe what his Authority Figures tell him he must believe.

In the nick of time, as the movie-studio-world is being auctioned off around them, Tirebiter Man and Boy confront one another. Realizing that they are the same person, and that they have both "Sold Out," the Lieutenant walks out of his movie and George (with a four-letter word) drops his load out of the TV.

Pastor Flash's sermon is over. George, like Babe, seems to have fallen asleep watching the TV. Awakened, he clicks it off. The phone rings. During the long night, all the great comic spirits have called on him, the answering service reports. But George is still ravenously hungry. The sound of an ice-cream truck in the distance distracts him. He opens his door to find birds singing in the early morning. To be outside restores his youth and he runs after the bells, having escaped at last.

don't crush that dwarf, hand me the pliers

AMBIENT SOUNDS: *Chairs scraping, mumbling, coughing as in a large hall. A* JANITOR *shuffles in and turns something on.*

JANITOR: You people got trouble here? Well, I don' know why you people seem to think this is magic. It's just this little chromium switch here . . . [*click*] My, you people are so superstitious . . .

SOUND: JANITOR *shuffling out and door closing. A generator comes on, builds in sound. An electric organ cuts in and out. The generator noise catches. The audience in the hall reacts to the catch, and applauds.*

VOICE: Well! My iron lung is working again . . .

SOUND: *A radio comes on somewhere, broadcasting the* REV MAURICE X NIGRA *and his congregation:*

REV M: Well, do you know about the gatherin'? I said, do you know about the gatherin'? I say the gatherin' of the Revolutionary Forces! Well, that's gonna be at Reverend Willie's pad—at three o'clock this afternoon—and be on time . . .

SOUNDS: *Men are searching for the radio. There is an exchange of voices and walkie-talkie radios:*

VOICE: What's that?

SECOND VOICE: One of those damn kids has got a radio!

WALKIE-TALKIE: Bob, this is Mobile Security Patrol One. There seems to be a young-type person in the audience with a Negro radio. Would you check that out please?

WALKIE TWO: We're checking it out, Bob.

WALKIE-TALKIE: Thank you, Bob.

SECOND VOICE: Over there, Larry!

SOUND: *Click of radio being turned off. Handclapping and applause. Voices shout from the audience:*

VOICE: Say it!

ANOTHER: Speak to us!

AND ANOTHER: Say it to me!

AND FOURTH VOICE: Let's hear from ya'!

SOUND: *Microphone feedback, tapping on the mike.*

REV MOUSE: . . . icrophone working? . . . Is it going to be all right?

AUDIENCE RESPONSE: It's gonna be all right!

REV MOUSE: Ha, ha, ho! You bet, Dear Friends, it is going to be all right. It's going to be all right tonight, here at the Powerhouse Church of the Presumptious Assumption of the Blinding Light.

SOUND: *Organ music swelling.*

LEROY [*singing*]: Oh, Blinding Light,
        Oh, Light that blinds,
        I cannot see,
        Look out for me!

SOUND: *Leroy falling over.*

REV MOUSE: Yes, Friends, welcome to Pastor Flash's Hour of Reckoning, with Organ Leroy at his organ again, and the Fifty-Voice St. Louis Aquarium Choir. I'm Deacon E.L. Mouse. But, Dear Friends, in these days of modern time, when you can't tell the ACs from the DCs, well, aren't we all yearning for someone who can turn on a little stopping power? Dear Friends, I mean a smokey glass. Don't you think I mean a lightning rod with which to chase these spooks away? Don't you know I mean our own Pastor Rod Flash! He's been up for a week, but he's coming down!

SOUND: *Distant B-29.*

FLASH [*on radio throughout*]: Hello, Dear Friends. It's so beautiful up here, Dear Friends. It's so clean. Yes. Dear Friends, there's no drunken drivers here. No broken glass. No air. Over.

REV MOUSE [*on radio*]: White Lightning, White Lightning, this is Ground Beef Control. Do you read me? Over.

FLASH: I read only Good Books. Over.

REV MOUSE: Ho, ho, ho! You must be way out there, Pastor. Over.

FLASH: I'm high, all right, but not on false drugs. I'm high on the real thing. Powerful gasoline, a clean windshield, and a shoeshine. Over.

REV MOUSE: He's turning over!

SOUNDS: *The airplane turning over and diving. Noise of fighting over the radio.*

FLASH [*off, excited*]: Get thee behind me!!

REV MOUSE: Are you in danger, Pastor?

FLASH [*coughing*]: I'm all right, Roger. Just a little argument with my co-pilot. And guess what, Rog? The little red needle's pointing to "E"—and, while that's always stood for Excellent in my Book, I guess it means I'm out of gas. You'll have to sing me in, my friends. My favorite. Hymn 1517. Aghh . . . [*fading*]

CHOIR [*singing*]: We're marching, marching to Shibboleth,
        With the Eagle and the Sword!
        We're praising Zion 'til her death,
        Until we meet our last reward!

MEN: Our Lord's reward!

WOMEN: Zion! Oh happy Zion!
        O'er wrapp'd, but not detained!

MEN: Lion! Oh frocious Lion!
        His beard our mighty mane!

WOMEN:	At First and Main!
MEN:	Oh, we'll go marching, marching to Omaha, With the Buckram and the Cord!
WOMEN:	You'll hear us "boom" our State!
MEN:	Ha, ha! As we cross the final ford!
WOMEN:	The flaming Ford!
CHOIR:	Zion! Oh mighty Zion! Your bison now are dust! As your cornflakes rise 'Gainst the rust-red skies, Then our blood requires us must Go . . .
MEN:	Marching, marching to Shibboleth, With the Eagle and the . . .
WOMEN:	The Buckram and the Cord!
MEN:	Sword! Praising Zion 'til her death!
WOMEN:	Ha, ha!
MEN:	Until we eat our last reward!
WOMEN:	The flaming Ford!
CHOIR:	Zion! Oh righteous Zion! There is no one to blame! For the homespun pies 'Neath the cracking skies Shall release the fulsome rain!
TENOR:	Shall release!
MEN:	Shall release!
SOPRANO:	Shall release!
WOMEN:	Shall release!
CHOIR:	Shall release the vinyl rein!

SOUNDS: *The airplane crash-lands.*

FLASH [*on PA*]: I'm down! Thank you, Dear Friends, I'm down, I'm grounded, safe and sound, trailing clouds of glory, I'm down. And I'm marching! Yes, Dear Friends, I'm marching to dinner! 'Cause Godamighty, I'm hungry! Yes! I'm hungry! Safe and sound and hungry!

AUDIENCE RESPONSE: We're hungry!

FLASH: Of course you're hungry! I'm hungry! We're all hungry! So let's eat!

AUDIENCE: Let's eat!

FLASH: And he said the word!

VOICE: What was it?

FLASH: And we ate it! Hot dog! And what was the word?

AUDIENCE: Hot Dog!

FLASH: Hot Dog! Yes, Dear Friends, a mighty Hot Dog is our Lord! I'm not talking about Hate! No, I'm talking about Ate! Dinner at Eight! Let's eat!

VOICE: More sugar!

FLASH [continues on the TV in the background]: Ah, the glories of food, the communication of communion. Ethyl and Rosenberg are passing among you with the plates. . . .

GEORGE [yawns, takes a toke]: Must be four o'clock in the morning. I sure am hungry. [Gropes around, opens refrigerator]

FLASH [under]: I want you to pick of those plates and eat of those condiments, then, I want you to fill your bodies and your mouths and your minds with the thoughts and realities of food. Dear Friends, Jesus said, "Let us be as children." And what do children do? They stuff themselves from day to night. They eat. They fill themselves with the reality of existence, my friends. The one common bond that holds the world together. The bond of food, the need for food, the void of emptiness. We must fill it and fill us with the fullness of it.

GEORGE [looking]: No cookies left . . . glass of green maraschino cherries . . . half a jar of mayonnaise . . . No! That's my mescaline . . . Laughing Cow Cheese . . . Jeezus! Boy is my mouth dry! [Walking back and turning up TV]

FLASH [under]: We must eat of our friends the birds, of our friends the cows, of our friends the pigs. Yes, it's good to eat a friend, my friend. And when the duck comes down with the magic word, what is the word?

GEORGE [yawns]: I'm so hungry. . . . There's nothing to eat here!

FLASH [under]: The word is "Food!" And we ate him. Eat! Eat!

SOUND: TV Click!

ARNIE BOHUNK [on TV]: . . . urrounded by a thin, thin 16-millimeter shell. And inside, it's delicious!

GEORGE [aside]: I'll bet.

ARNIE: That's Arnie's Whole Beef Halves—We Deliver. Thirsty?

GEORGE: That's me!

ARNIE: Wouldn't you like some of this Old Filipino Creemy, comin' in shorts and quarts?

GEORGE: Yeah!

ARNIE: And tubs of slaw.

GEORGE: Gimme two.

ARNIE: Sorry, only one Tub per family. That's Whole Beef Halves—We Deliver. Everywhere.

LOCAL ANNOUNCER: Offer not good after curfew in Sectors R or N.

GEORGE: They never come up into the hills, those guys.

SOUND: News teletype on TV.

NEWS ANNOUNCER: This is the Hour of the Wolf News. Big Light Slated to Appear in East. Sonic Booms Scare Minority Groups in Sector B. And there's Hamburger All Over The Highway in Mystic, Connecticut.

NEWSCASTER: Good morning. Those are the headlines; now, the rumors behind the news. Here, in a satellite report bounced from Com Symp III is reporter Felix Papparazzi.

GEORGE: Aw, who needs the headlines?

SOUND: *He turns down the TV and begins flipping through the Yellow Pages. The Newscast continues under.*

FELIX: Here at General Hersey General Hospital the most remarkable medical achievement of modern times, America's first man-made baby, Adam one-three, is developing far beyond the expectations of Surrogate General Klein and his medical staff. Dr. General, sir, how is Adam 13 progressing?

GEORGE [*mumbling*]: Let's see . . . Ocelots. Paupers. Pipe-nipples, Polombras, Pizzas! Armenian Gardens . . . Hank's Juggernaut . . . New Leviathan . . . Nick's Swell . . .

SOUND: *He picks up the phone and dials. The Newscast goes on:*

KLEIN: We are quite frankly astonished at the rate of cellular progression.

FELIX: I realize that antiseptic security precautions must be maintained, but when will we be able to actually see him?

KLEIN: Surely not before his growth rate stabilizes.

FELIX: How many inches is he now?

KLEIN: As of an hour ago—148. That's lunar feet. He has a full head of hair, his features are normal in every respect, and pleasing, too, I might add. Our only concern now is with a certain pigmentation-imbalance which has manifested all day.

GEORGE [*phoning*]: Uh, this is George Tirebiter, Camden N 200 R. [*Pause*] Uh, I want to order a pizza to go and no anchovies. [*Pause*] What? [*Clicks phone*] Oh, man! Nobody will come up here at all! [*He turns up the TV*]

FELIX: Is that serious, Doctor General?

KLEIN: No, not serious. It's a matter of personal taste.

NEWSCASTER: Adam Thirteen's incipient negritude will come as a pleasant surprise to his honorary Aquarian Parents, Ralph Bunche and Ida Lupino.

GEORGE: Yeah, I'll bet it will!

NEWSCASTER: In other news, final steps were taken in or near Washington to secure the merger of the US Government with TMZ General Corp. This former zinc bushing . . .

GEORGE: Enough!

SOUND: *He* Clicks! *past three empty channels back to* PASTOR FLASH:

FLASH: Come on up here, if you want to eat! Come on up, darling. Don't be afraid. I won't bite you!

GEORGE [*watching*]: Oh, that's weird. Weird. Too much!

FLASH: Is it too much, friends? (Pull the curtains, Fred.) Look at this, look at this steaming heap. Too much of Admirable Bird's crackly brown French-fried Chicken Fingers? Too many cuts of Mother Baker's Deep-Dish Sheep Dip Cherrystone Pie? Too many Tubs Of Slaw?

GEORGE: Far out. Oh, it really looks good! Oh, no, man. I want more!

FLASH: Then take some, friends. Dip deep, darlings! Take some pot-buttered groat clusters!

GEORGE: OK, man, you've been talkin' a lot. Hand 'em over!

FLASH: Here you are!

SOUND: *Food coming right out of the TV.*

GEORGE: What? Oh, well! My God, it's still warm!

FLASH: Say thank you, friends!

GEORGE: They're covered with . . . Thank you. This is amazing!

FLASH: Say thank you!

GEORGE: Thank you, thank you!

FLASH: Not with your mouth full. I'll talk. You eat.

GEORGE: OK, I'm eating, I'm eating.

FLASH: And while you eat, be assured, Dear Friends, that one of the Two Greatest Guys in the Universe, that Great Guy Upstairs, is thanking me, as you are thanking me.

GEORGE: Thank you. Thank you . . .

FLASH: Doesn't that change your heart, friends?

GEORGE: Certainly does!

FLASH: Don't you feel your heart burning?

GEORGE: Oh, I can feel it!

FLASH: Can you feel the change? Are you full? Don't you feel the Changes, Dear Friends?

GEORGE: Right on, Daddy-o!

FLASH: Are you changing, friend? Isn't he . . .

GEORGE: Yes, I am ch . . .

SOUND: *The TV sound becomes full stereo, full screen.*

JERRY YARROW: . . . anging with the times. So let's meet him!

SOUND: *Light organ music.*

K'EN: Well, Jerry, our next famous Fall Guy is still putting his art in cans from Canada to Kashmir. Winner of the Academy's coveted Good Sport Award in 1956 for Excellence in Hollywood, meet George Leroy Tire-biter!

SOUND: *Applause. Organ theme ends.*

JERRY: Hubba, hubba, George! What a suit! Well, it's nice to see you looking like you're back on your feet again, George, and ready to play our little game again.

GEORGE: Thank you very much.

JERRY: George, first a tip for our viewers, maybe. How does an old man like you stay alive?

GEORGE: Well sir, I try to get up every morning and watch television all day, Mr. Yarrow.

GERRY: Do you have a special diet, George?

GEORGE: I don't eat.

JERRY: You don't eat?

GEORGE: No. But it hasn't affected my appetite! Heh heh heh!

JERRY: Well, George—it hasn't affect . . . ha ha ha!

GEORGE: You don't have any little groat clusters I could chew on do you?

JERRY: Later, George! You won't want to eat in a minute, after you turn your back and get ready for this Stab From The Past!

SOUND: *Organ theme music.*

GEORGE: Oh, my!

JERRY: All right, George. Now, you remember all those loveable, stupid Peorgie & Mudhead movies you were responsible for?

GEORGE: My goodness, I haven't seen any of those in years.

JERRY: Well, Georgie, what are you going to do when the original "Bottles," Mudhead's crazy, hopped-up girl friend, drops right through that Celebrity Trap Door?

GEORGE: Oh, no! That woman's trying to kill me! . . .

SOUND: *TV* Click!

BOB BASELINE: . . . et's talk about your car. It's screaming "Wash me, please!" Now, if you're a Mr. Common Sense, you won't believe me when I tell you that I've got an envelope that'll clean your car while you're driving it home to work. Well, George, believe me this time, because this one isn't like the Austrian self-sharpening razors. No, friends, no overheating like the tropical fishes. No zizzing and dripping like with the dike . . .

SOUND: *TV* Click!

KATHY: . . . ey don't want it any more, Dr. Gunderson!

DOC: Don't want what, child?

KATHY: My coffee! The warden says he's tired of my coffee.

DOC: It's ban pretty clear dat your coffee don't got Zest Appeal.

KATHY: Zest Appeal? What's that?

DOC: I don't know . . .

KATHY: Ohh . . . [*sobs*]

DOC: Dat's the secret ingredient in Ersatz Brothers Coffee, ya! Look here. A blend of the finest Brazilian Soya Beans, Chilean Chicory Nuts and Spanish Flies. Here, take this can home with you, Katie . . .

ANNOUNCER: The next morning . . .

KATHY: More coffee, warden?

WARDEN: No . . . I think I've had enough . . .

KATHY: Ah . . . !

ANNOUNCER: Erzatz Brothers Coffee. The Real One! Look for the can in the plain brown can.

SOUND: *TV Click!*

GEORGE: . . . not in any way want to put myself in a confrontatory position either with the United Snakes, or with Them. And you can believe me, because I never lie and I'm always right. So wake up! [*slap and baby crying*] And take a look at your only logical choice. Me. George Tirebiter.

VOICE OVER: Paid for by the Tirebiter For Political Solutions Committee, Sector R.

STAFF ANNOUNCER: This is UTV—For You—The Viewer.

SOUND: *Theme music.*

TAPED ANNOUNCER: The Howl of the Wolf Movie! Presenting honest stories of working people, as told by rich Hollywood stars.

SOUND: *Wolf howl.*

STAFF ANNOUNCER: This morning's wacky feature, Peorgie and Mudhead in "Highschool Madness," with Dave Casman as Peorgie and Joe Bertman as Mudhead . . .

SOUND: *Movie fanfare music.*

ANDROID SISTERS [*singing*]:
> "Peorgie Tirebiter!
> He's a spy and a girl delighter!
> Orgie Firefighter!
> He's a student like you!
> If you're looking for a Captain of the Ringball Team,
> You can bet he won't be there!
> You'll find him pa-popping off at Pop's Sodium Shoppe,
> Tr-trailing a Red with red hair!
> Doobie doo wah . . .
> Peorgie Tirebiter!
> Just a student like you!"

PEORGIE: Like me?

ANDROID SISTERS: "Just a student like you!"

DAD: Stop singing and finish your homework!

ANDROID SISTERS: "Just a student like you! ooooooooo . . ."

SOUND: *Clatter of dishes.*

MOM [*humming, then calls*]: Adolf! Come and get it! Your clam cakes are getting damp!

DAD [*calling from outside*]: 10-4 Eleanor! [*Door slams and he enters*] Whew! Defoliating a Victory Garden certainly does work up an appetite!

MOM: You sit down, Father, and dig right in!

DAD: That's right! This afternoon, I'll be able to start digging the pit. If I can

get some work out of that boy of yours, I can have the bunker finished
by Election Day. Where is Peorgie, anyway?

MOM: He's up in his room, helping Porcelain make the bed.

SOUND: *Bedsprings squeeking.*

PEORGIE: [*Panting*]

PORCELAIN: Oh, Peorgie, oh, my, my, my!!

MOM [*off*]: Peorgie! Peorgie Tirebiter!

PEORGIE: Co—co—coming, Mother!

MOM [*on mike*]: He's so good with the servants, Fred.

DAD: Stop calling me Fred. My name's Adolf.

SOUND: *Running down stairs.*

PEORGIE: Bombs away, Dad! Morning, Mom! Hot Dog! Groat cakes again! Heavy on the 30-weight, Mom.

DAD: Don't eat with your hands, son. Use your entrenching tool.

PEORGIE: Aw, gee, Dad! I'm just trying to save time. It isn't every day a guy graduates from High School!

DAD: How many times have I heard that before?

MOM: Well, you boys fight it out among yourselves.

DAD: OK, Mother.

SOUND: *Fighting and punching.*

MOM: Oh, my, my. Look at the time. I've got to dress for my bridge club.

PEORGIE [*winded*]: Gee, Mom! Isn't that bridge built yet?

DAD: No, Son! [*Punches him*] And it won't be, until free hands on both sides of the Big Ditch can press the same button at the same time. [*Punch*]

PEORGIE: OK, Dad! I give! Ow! Oh, boy. Can I eat my breakfast now?

DAD: Only if you stay out of trouble, boy. Your shenanigans could cost me this election.

PEORGIE: Aw, come on, Dad. No Irishman can stop you from getting to be Dog Killer this time. You're a natural!

MOM: Don't wolf your food.

SOUND: *Car horn toots.*

PEORGIE: Oh oh! There's Mudhead! Graduation, here I come! So long, Dad! Keep 'em flying!

SOUND: *He runs out, slamming the door.*

DAD: Oh, that son of mine . . .

MOM: He's not your son, Fred.

DAD: Stop torturing me, Ethyl!

SOUND: *Old car driving away. Motor in background.*

PEORGIE: Come on, step on it, Mudhead!

MUDHEAD: Aw, I'd love to, Peorgie, but I've got my two-tones through the floorboard already!

PEORGIE: Well, OK. Then we could take the shortcut through Frogtown!

MUDHEAD: Aw reet! We can stop off at Pop's and dig some jugs!

PEORGIE: Some what?

MUDHEAD: That Louise Wong's got a balcony you could do Shakespeare from!

PEORGIE: Aw, not now, Mudhead. They need me at the last meeting of the Philatelist's Club.

MUDHEAD: I didn't know you masturbated.

PEORGIE: Aw, creepies, Mudhead! Where's your school spirit?

MUDHEAD: In the rumble seat. Want a snort?

PEORGIE: Very funny.

MUDHEAD: Sure is.

PEORGIE: Gee, everybody at Morse Science High has an extra-curricular activity but you.

MUDHEAD: Doesn't Louise count?

PEORGIE: Only to ten, Mudhead. You know, that's just it.

MUDHEAD: Just what?

PEORGIE: Well, we're the leaders of tomorrow.

MUDHEAD: Yeah, but it's today.

PEORGIE: But what are you going to do tomorrow, after we graduate?

MUDHEAD: Oh, well, I thought maybe I'd go out and find a bunch of guys who dress alike and follow 'em around.

PEORGIE: What?

MUDHEAD: Or, I could go pick up a couple of girls!

PEORGIE: Oh, is that all you think about? Picking up things? Gollee, Mudhead! Don't you remember what Principal Poop put down at the Pep Rally yesterday?

MUDHEAD: Principal who . . . . ?

SOUND: *Car crossfades with marching band and cheerleaders in an auditorium.*

CHEERLEADERS: P-E-P-E-P!!
>Mo-oooo-re Pep Pills!
>Pep Pills! Pep Pills! Pep Pills!
>[*Faster and faster*] Yaaay! Pep Pills!

POOP [*taps on microphone*]: Is this on? Thank you, fellow kids. [*Aside, to band*] Quiet! . . . In addressing for the assembling this morning . . .

ALVARADO [*in audience*]: Fuck you!

POOP: Thank you. Er, I am recalling the words of the foundry—er—founder of Morse Science High School, Ukaipah Heap, who pressed the first bricks with his own hands . . .

ALVARADO: Who cares?

POOP: "Knowledge for the pupil—the people," he said. "Give them a light and they'll follow it anywhere." We think that is a fair and wise guy— er—rule to be guided by . . .

ALVARADO: What is reality?

POOP: And we're not afraid of it, are we?

ALVARADO: Eat it!

POOP: You bet!

ALVARADO: Eat it raw!

POOP: Rah, rah, rah! That's the spirits we have here! So come on, kids!

ALVERADO: Fuck you!

POOP: Line up, sign up, and re-enlist today! Because we need more schooling for more students for Morse Science High!

ALVARADO: Boooo!

POOP: Thank you.

ALVARADO: Boooooo!

POOP [*fading off*]: Fuck you, too!

SOUND: *Car driving crossfades under.*

PEORGIE: So ya see, Mudhead? It's like the Pooper said. With counter-subversive educational priorities the way they are, well, it really helps our side to re-enlist.

MUDHEAD: Is that what you're gonna do?

PEORGIE: Aw, hell no! Right after I graduate, I'm gonna cut the soles off my shoes, sit in a tree, and learn to play the flute!

MUDHEAD: Hey! Look, Peorgie!

SOUND: *Car screeches to a halt.*

PEORGIE: Hey, watch it!

MUDHEAD: Where are you gonna graduate from?

PEORGIE: Holy Mudhead, Mackerel! Morse Science High! It's disappeared!

SOUND: *Musical Fanfare becoming jerky and garbled and cutting out.*

[End of side one]

SOUND: *Music cutting in and out as someone pounds on the TV set.*

STAFF ANNOUNCER: Technical difficulties are preventing the continuation of tonight's Foxhowl Feature, "Highschool Madness." We are working on the problem . . .

COMMERCIAL VOICES: Shoes For Industry! Shoes For The Dead! Shoes For Industry!

JOE: Hi! I'm Joe Beets. Say, what chance does a returning deceased war veteran have for that good-paying job, more sugar and the free mule you've been dreaming of? Well, think it over. Then take off your shoes. Now you can see how increased spending opportunities means harder work for everyone, and more of it, too! So do your part today, Joe. Join with millions of your neighbors and turn in your shoes!

COMMERCIAL VOICE: For Industry!

SOUND: *Hubbub of voices under.*

SOUVENIR **NEW CHINATOWN**
1970 LOS ANGELES, CALIF.

SOUVENIR **NEW CHINATOWN**
1970 LOS ANGELES, CALIF.

MUDHEAD: Jumpin' Jujubees, Peorgie! It looks like a wasteland! There's nothing left but the flagpole!

PEORGIE: I don't know what to say, Mudhead. I . . .

BOTTLES: Hi, Mudhead!

MUDHEAD: Oh, hi, Bottles.

BOTTLES: I know who did this! It was those bullies at Communist Martyrs High School, that's who!

PEORGIE: Oh, come on, Bottles. We don't know who did it yet.

BOTTLES: I have a very good idea . . .

ALVARADO: Hey, Peorgie, you're a white man, you've got to help us!

PICO: Yeah, right!

ALVARADO: What—what do you think—what do you think we ought to—what do you think we should do?

PICO: Speak English, Alvarado!

PEORGIE: Well, gee, I don't think we should jump to any conclusions or take a . . .

PICO: Hey, Peorgie! Principal Poop's on the radio! Turn on the car radio! Poop's on!

MUDHEAD: What are all these Mexicans doing here?

PEORGIE: Shhh! Gather round, kids, and stay on camera. We'll all listen together!

MUDHEAD: Take it easy now!

SOUND: *Radio tuning through static.*

POOP [*on radio*]: All of us want to know, just as much as I want to know, who's responsible . . .

BOTTLES: Communist Martyrs High School, that's who . . .

PEORGIE: Shhh!

POOP [*continuing*]: And until we do, I must make my dirty—er—duty clean—clear. Ahem. And announce the suspendering of the upcoming graduating exercises which cannot—and will—which aren't taking place!

PEORGIE: Oh, no! I'm never gonna get out of here!

POOP: But don't worry, don't worry. Your food, housing, insecurity will be guaranteed by your Department of Redundancy Department, and the Natural Guard.

MUDHEAD: Hey! They're gonna surround us!

POOP: And remember, trusswrappers will be persecuted. So please, stay where you are. Don't move. And don't panic. Don't take off your shoes. Jobs is on the way!

PEORGIE: Gollee!

POOP [*fading*]: Thank you. Now, here's a record I think you'll really dig . . .

PEORGIE: Hold it! Hey, hold it down, kids. Hold it down. Don't get excited!

PICO: Who's excited?

PEORGIE: Listen, the only way we're gonna get the school back is us! I've got a really swell ide . . .

STAFF ANNOUNCER [*after a pause*]: I'm sorry. We have lost the picture portion of our pic-smission. However, we will continue with the soun . . .

SOUND: *TV* Click!

DR MATH: . . . at's 2 Postmen, times 3 Animal Control Officers, divided by 2 Gassed Meter Readers, makes how many Bendable Integrated Community Workers? Decode your answer now.

SOUND: *Music and effects.*

DR MATH: Did you remember to carry the Bum? Good! The answ . . .

SOUND: *TV* Click!

SAILOR BILL: OK, kids! And we have another letter here from our Happy Birthday Gu-gu-gu-gumdropper in Sector R. It's little Sally I. Chink—er, uh—Ching! And she's 12 years old today. Well, that's wonderful, Sally! You're going to start menstruating soon, huh? Don't you think you ought to be . . .

SOUND: *TV* Click!

PATTY: . . . that's why he's so mean! [*Laughing*]

HUGH: [*Laughs*]

PATTI: Oh, well, yes, yes. Well, what else happened in history today, Hugh?

HUGH: In history, Patti, well, today of course is the 38th of Cunegonde, and on this day in 1-9-3-8-B-C, Patti—Mr. George Antrobus invented the wheel.

PATTI: And just in time!

HUGH: And in 1889, the Peace of Humus broke out, ending the Hundred-Year's War against the Cows.

PATTI: Yup.

HUGH: And last year, Patti, you and the viewers will be interested in noting that the world ended.

PATTI: As we know it, Hugh.

HUGH: You're darn tootin', Patti.

PATTI: I sure am.

HUGH: Say, who was born today?

PATTI: Nobody, Hugh.

HUGH: I mean in history, Patti. Before they changed the water . . .

SOUND: *TV* Click! *Wind blowing. Distant cannonfire.*

PRIVATE [*whispering*]: Hey! Hey, Sarge!

SGT MUDHEADSKI: Yeah?

PRIVATE: How long have Pico and Alvarado been out on patrol?

SGT M: Since 1400.

PRIVATE: Geee! That's 2000 years!

ANOTHER PVT: I hope they can find their way back. I'm gettin' hungry . . .

SOUND: *Airplane buzzes them.*

SGT M: Hit the dirt!

PRIVATE: Was that one of ours?

ANOTHER PVT: Yeah. Beans. Last of the beans.

PRIVATE: I'm so tired of Chinese food.

LT TIREBITER [*off*]: Hey, Sergeant Mudheadski! Come over here. We got a problem.

SGT M [*walking over*]: Yeah, what is it, Lieutenant Tirebiter?

LT TIREBITER: Silverberg here won't go over Pork Chop Hill.

SILVERBERG [*off*]: Killin' pigs ain't Kosher, Sarge.

SGT M: Can the wise lips, Silverberg. None of us ain't goin' nowhere until that patrol gets back.

SILVERBERG [*fading*]: Talk, talk, talk . . .

SGT M: Personally, I'm worried about Pico and Alvarado.

LT TIREBITER: Well, don't make a "Korea" out of it! Ha ha ha!

SGT M: Don't let it get to you, Lieutenant.

LT TIREBITER: I'm alright, Mudheadski. Listen, those good boys found their way out of East L.A., they can find their way back into this Gook Valley, right?

PRIVATE: Sarge, Sarge! Somethin's moving out in the woods!

SGT M: Where?

PRIVATE: Sector N.

LT TIREBITER: OK, give 'em the password, Sarge.

SGT M: Yeah. I better disguise my voice. Heya Joe! Who wonna Seconda Worlda War, you so smart!

PICO [*calling*]: Not responsible!

ALVARADO [*off*]: Park and lock it!

SGT M: It's OK, Sir. That's Pico and Alvarado.

LT TIREBITER: Aw right.

SGT M: Come on in, boys! Hey, hey! Don't run in the trenches!

ALVARADO: Hi, you guys!

SGT M: Watch out for that entrenching tool!

SOUND: *Crash of men and equipment.*

LT TIREBITER: Aw right. Stand easy, men.

PICO: Help me up!

LT TIREBITER: How was it out there?

PICO: Weird! We been shootin' reds and yellows all day.

ALVARADO: Hoo boy! Am I sleepy!

LT TIREBITER: What about the Gooks?

PICO: Bad news, Lieutenant. There're gooks all around here.

ALVARADO: They live here, Lieutenant. They got women and pigs and gardens and everything.

PICO: I was talking to this one little gook . . .

ALVARADO: I was talkin' to his daughter! She's got the biggest . . .

LT TIREBITER: That's swell, Corporal, but we got orders to surround these little gooks.

ALVARADO: That'll be easy, Leftenant. There's millions of them on all three sides of us.

LT TIREBITER: That means we've got those little gooks right where we want them, right?

PICO: Yeah, yeah! And tonight's the planting moon, so every one of them is going to be out wading in the paddies.

ALVARADO: Me too!

SGT M: This sounds like a perfect set-up. What are we gonna do, Lieutenant?

PICO: What *are* we gonna do, Lieutenant?

ALVARADO: *What* are we gonna do, Lieutenant?

LT TIREBITER: All right, men. We're gonna deploy at 0800.

SGT M: Check!

LT TIREBITER: Recon all L.O.M. Sectors.

SGT M: Czech!

LT TIREBITER: Bring up the 455s.

SGT M: Pole!

LT TIREBITER: Locate our fire perimeters.

SGT M: Bohunk!

LT TIREBITER: Make a clean sweep. Flush out the enemy and ki-ki-ki-um . . .

SGT M: What's that, sir?

ALVARADO: Sir? Lieutenant, excuse me, sir, what are we gonna do, man?

PICO: Yeah, after we flush 'em out?

LT TIREBITER: We're gonna lock and load, Private, and we're gonna go out there and ki . . .

ALVARADO: Hey, man! What are we gonna do, man?

PICO: What'll we do when we lock and load?

LT TIREBITER: We're gonna ki-ki-ki . . .

SGT M: Take it easy. It's not your fault, Peorgie! Come on, Peorgie!

LT TIREBITER: Ki-ki-ki . . .

SOUND: *TV* Clicks! *past two empty channels.*

FATHER: . . . tetrics with Nurse Warren. Don't you remember what I told you at the lake last summer?

SON: Gee, Dad . . .

LOUDSPEAKER VOICE: Will the real Dr. Pederman please report to Neurosurgery immediately?

SON: Dad, I told you I was sorry then, and I'm sorry now.

FATHER: Does Peggy know that?

SON: Who's Peggy?

SOUND: *Organ theme music in and under.*

ANNOUNCER: We'll return to "The Painful Threshold" after this message.

COMMERCIAL VOICE OVER: Comedienne Mrs. Arlene Yukamoto of Pine Barren, New Jersey, doesn't know our Napalmolive camera is focused on her!

MRS Y: No. It's true. You see—my husband is a policeman, and you wouldn't believe how dirty he gets my clothes. I mean it. It's unbelievable.

VOICE OVER: Oh, but we believed Mrs. P.Q. and listen to her reaction.

MRS Y: I worry about it all night sometimes, you know? I hate to admit it. Look at this horrible stain. Sometimes I think my kids are doing it on purpose.

SOUND: *Little siren and drum-beats.*

SGT S: Nothin's on purpose, ma'am!

MRS Y: Who are you?

SGT S: Sergeant Schvincter of the Dirt Patrol! Our mission, to keep America clean. And when the job gets this dirty, there's only one weapon! New Napalmolive, with enzy . . .

SOUND: *TV* Click!

MADGE: . . . esident of the World Bank, and you still find the time to make the nicest peccary pie in all of Lompox! Oh, Darlene! I remember when the least little problem used to put you right to sleep!

DARLENE: Not any more, Madge. Today's Modern-Now-A-Go-Go woman just pops these simple little pills called Angerdream . . .

SOUND: *TV* Click!

COP: Swell demonstration, eh, Sarge?

SARGE: It's routine.

COP: Maybe. But if the Chief ever caught me takin' these pills he'd snap my head off!

SARGE: Here, try one of mine.

COP: Oh, yeah?

SARGE: Yeah. The Chief himself's been on these for a week, and he's a changed . . .

SOUND: *TV* Click! *Followed by Theme Music.*

HIND: . . . and welcome, Dear Friends, to the wonderful world of snails and adventure, as we board the Golden Hind.

SOUND: *Theme music out.*

HIND: Hello, friends. I'm Bob Hind, and today . . .

SOUND: *TV* Clicks!

MUDHEAD: . . . That was a stupid idea, Peorgie! Here we are at Commie Martyrs, but how are we gonna find Morse Science High?

PEORGIE: Well, let's get out of Exposition Park, Mudhead, and we'll be all right. Come on this way.

MUDHEAD: You go first. Stop shoving . . .

SOUND: *They go through a door into an echoing hall.*

MUDHEAD: Hey, Peorgie?

PEORGIE: What?

MUDHEAD: I ain't afraid, but it sure is sp-sp-spooky in here!

PEORGIE: That's because we're on the Other Side.

MUDHEAD: Yeah, must be. Hey! What's that?

PEORGIE [*startled*]**:** What! Oh, it's OK. It's just a picture, Mudhead. Let go of my pants.

MUDHEAD: Peorge . . . ?

PEORGIE: What?

MUDHEAD: I'm not holding on to your pants!

PEORGIE: You're not?

MUDHEAD: Noooo!

PEORGIE: Oh, nooooo!

BOTTLES: Hi, boys!

PEORGIE: Oh, Bottles! How did you get in here?

BOTTLES: Oh, I have my ways.

MUDHEAD: I bet you gave the guard a sleeve job!

BOTTLES: Oh yeah? That's what you guys are always thinking about.

PEORGIE: Quiet!

BOTTLES: You just come over here and I'll show you something.

MUDHEAD: Don't you trust her, Peorgie. Then she'll want to see yours!

PEORGIE: No, Mudhead. She's right. Look!

BOTTLES: You see? You see what I found?

MUDHEAD: By golly, it's him!

PEORGIE: They've got the big portrait of principal Poop that used to hang in the Boy's Supreme Court at Morse Science!

MUDHEAD: Those eyes! Weird!

SOUND: *Whistling and approaching footsteps.*

PEORGIE: Shh! It's one of them! I'll carry the ball. You guys be quiet.

BOTTLES: Shh! Be quiet. Shh!

MUDHEAD: Be cool, Peorge! Be cool!

ALVARADO: Hiya, kiddo!

PEORGIE: Er—Shoes For Industry, Compadre.

ALVARADO: Yeah, sure. Are you guys holding?

PEORGIE: Gosh, no. The means of production are held by all the people.

ALVARADO: No, man. You know, you got any uppers?

PEORGIE: Uppers? No. There are no classes in our society.

MUDHEAD: Or in our High School!

BOTTLES: Quiet, stupid.

ALVARADO: Hey, come on, baby, you can tell me! You got any pot?

PEORGIE: Oh, not yet. But soon heavy industry will make it possible for all the people to have everything it desires in a free marketplace.

BOTTLES: That's right, yes.

ALVARADO: Oh, daddy-o, you guys are so crazy! [*Walking off*] Crazy, man, crazy! Crazy, man, crazy! What are you gonna do . . .

MUDHEAD: Gosh! You really convinced him we were OK, Comrade—er—I mean, Peorgie.

BOTTLES: That sure was a close one. We better get out of here.

PEORGIE: No, no, no. Wait a minute, Bottles. They must be hiding Morse Science around here someplace. They got the Pooper's picture.

MUDHEAD: They got everybody's picture.

BOTTLES: Well, they're not gonna get mine. I'm leaving.

PEORGIE: Hey, wait a minute. Not through there. That's got a flashing red light!

MUDHEAD: Hey, Bottles!

BOTTLES: Come on, guys!

SOUND: *Door opening.*

PEORGIE: Gee, now we'll have to go in after her! Come on, Mudhead.

MUDHEAD: OK. All right . . .

SOUND: *Walking through the door and shutting it.*

PEORGIE: Mudhead! We've found it!

MUDHEAD: Wow! Our old Alma Mater. It's been taken apart, and stacked up, and labeled!

PEORGIE: This has never happened to any other high school ever before!

MUDHEAD [*off*]: Hey, Peorgie, look at this big thing over here.

PEORGIE: What's that?

MUDHEAD: I dunno. It's got a label, though. I'll read it. Number 11478, Mural, Auditorium, Right Rear. "Heroic Struggle of the Little Guys to Finish the Mural."

PEORGIE: That's ours, all right. I guess we got 'em red-handed.

MUDHEAD: Yeah. Here's a red hand!

PEORGIE: Listen, I'll just take . . . *this* along for evidence and we'll go back . . .

DAD: Hold it right there, boys!

MUDHEAD: Mr. Tirebiter!

PEORGIE: Dad!

DAD: "Dad, sir" to you, son. I'm People's Commissioner Tirebiter, now. And nobody's sweetheart!

SOUND: *He punches Peorgie.*

PEORGIE [*reeling*]: Owl! You must have won the election, Dad!

DAD: Right, son. Now I *am* the people. And The People—US—wants me to tell them—It—just what you're doing with your hands in Number 35729 comma Shorts comma One Pair Blue Gym comma W/slash Protector, worn by Barbara Bobo!

PEORGIE: Oh, no!

SOUND: *Music under scene crossfades to crowd noises and the banging of a gavel.*

BAILIFF [*off*]: Oyez, Oyez! All rise for the courtroom scene! Take one!

PEORGIE: I'd like to take one, too, Dad!

DAD: Scared, son? Don't be. I love you at times like this.

PEORGIE: I know, Dad. But how can you be in—I mean—I still don't see how you can be my defense lawyer and the People's Prosecutor all at the same time.

DAD: Easy, son. This way I can personally see that you're persecuted to the full extent of the laws.

PEORGIE: That's my Dad!

BAILIFF: Will George Leroy Tirebiter please take the stand?

PEORGIE: Does he mean me?

DAD: Now, stand tall, Peorge. There's no . . . [*fading out*]

SOUND: *Commercial music.*

COMMERCIAL ANNOUNCER: This is a line of Indians leaving beautiful Rancho Malario—to make room for you! Here's the beautiful Trail of Tears Golf Course . . .

SOUND: *TV* Click! *White noise. Another* Click!

DANNY DOLLAR: . . . issis Caroline Presky, you've Sold Out!

SOUND: *Laughter, applause and happy organ theme.*

DANNY: Now, let's see just what you've won on this, your third day on Hawaiian Sell-Out! Bob, what's Mrs. Presky's heap so far?

BOB: Right, Jack! So far, a complete broken set of color bars for Mrs. P's new home, some levelled mountain skis and water-rollers for that fun-filled open season, an unattached Grid-Five Stand-Up Reheater with a smoke window, and now . . .

SOUND: *Audience gasps.*

DANNY: Three hundred full pounds of Chef Antoine's Southern Fried Glimps, toasted to golden perfection, cubed, reheated, and returned to water before you're ready, Mrs. P. And the inside? Well, look at that! It's just as lovely. Two shelves where none are needed. And look at that! Close the door and the light stays on!

SOUND: *Audience applause.*

DANNY: Well, how do you feel, Mrs. Presky?

MRS P: Ah—er—sick . . .

DANNY: Well, you can afford it now, love! But, like the Good Book says,

SOUND: *TV Click!*

KLEIN: Was that the line you took, Lieutenant?

MAJOR: You have to answer this one . . .

LT TIREBITER: I can't . . . I can't remember, sir. I told him twenty times, I can't remember.

MAJOR: Calm down, my boy. Our entire defense rests on you knowin . . .

KLEIN: Major! Kindly instruct your client to stop acting. And you could take a couple of lessons in military toughness yourself!

MAJOR: Yes, sir.

LT TIREBITER: Listen, everything went black. I have no way of knowing . . .

MAJOR: General, I must insist this man is in no condition to replay that inci . . .

KLEIN: Well, I can see that, Major. Will the recording Sergeant read the scene back to him?

SGT M: Yes sir. "Alvarado: Sir, what are we gonna do, man? Mudheadski: Take it easy, Lieutenant. Tirebiter: We're gonna go out there and ki-ki-ki-cut!! I can't say it. I'm sorry, but I . . . zzzzzzzt. Beep!"

KLEIN: Can you remember now, Lieutenant?

LT TIREBITER: Surrogate General Klein, sir. When I signed my contract with you, I fully intended to fulfill its terms with honor, sir. But you never told me I had to go out there and kill anybody. I . . .

KLEIN [*banging gavel*]: Lieutenant, we will not tolerate the use of prohibited language in this courts-martials. The accursed will be advised of the absence of his rights under the Secret Code of Military Toughness and will act accordingly.

SOUND: *Courtroom audience reaction.*

PEORGIE: Aw, gee whiz! I'm sorry!

DAD: I suppose it's we parents who should be sorry, Judge. We failed somewhere. We didn't raise this boy to use language like that.

JUDGE: It's not our fault anymore, Mr. Prosecution. Call the next witness.

DAD: What do you think I ought to call him, Judge?

JUDGE: Well, I don't know. We don't have a name for him. He never went to school.

DAD: Well, then, the People calls to the stand—you!

SOUND: *Confused murmur in the courtroom.*

PICO: Don't point at me, daddy-o, or I'll cut off your finger!

DAD: No, no. No, the second man from the rear. Over there. You. The man with no shoes!

MUDHEAD: Who, me?

DAD: You!

PEORGIE: Mudhead?? Gollee, Dad!

SOUND: *Gavel bangs. Crowd shushes.*

BAILIFF: You promise to covet property, propriety, plurality, surety, security, and not hurt the State? Say "what?"

MUDHEAD: What?

BAILIFF: Take your stand.

DAD: Now, then, Mr.—er—Head . . .

MUDHEAD: Hi, Mr. Tirebiter. You know me!

DAD: Do you know the defendant?

MUDHEAD: Do I know Peorgie?

DAD: And you spend all your free time with him?

MUDHEAD: Sure! Except when he's in school.

DAD: So you don't go to school?

MUDHEAD: Heck no. I'm thirty years old.

DAD: But you were in school, weren't you?

MUDHEAD: Never!

DAD: And with your friend Peorgie?

MUDHEAD: No!

DAD: Last night!

MUDHEAD: Oh! You mean Commie Martyrs!

DAD: Communist Martyrs High School, exactly!

MUDHEAD: Well, yeah. Of course. Peorgie had to find out where they were hiding Morse Science, or he couldn't get out!

DAD: Or he couldn't get out! He admits it. He was trying to get out!

MUDHEAD: Isn't everybody?

DAD: Yes! To Get Out in times of Declared Emergency!

PEORGIE: What emergency?

DAD: Well, there you are, Judge Poop. Youth here doesn't seem to know about the disappearance of the Old School!

MUDHEAD: But that's what Peorgie was lookin' for!

SOUND: *Gavel bangs to shush audience.*

JUDGE: If you don't answer the question, young man, we're going to have to gag you.

MUDHEAD: What question?

JUDGE: Gag him!

DAD: Who was that lady I saw you with last night?

MUDHEAD: Aww, that was no lady. That was Bottles.

KLEIN: Bottles?

LT TIREBITER: I got so I'd drink anything. After that I couldn't seem to get off the stuff. My whole career went up in smoke. There was no way I could follow the scenario written by the people who pay for your wheelchairs, General!

KLEIN: Are you impugning, sir, that this uniform might be for sale? This uniform that bears the three stars that indicate my ratings? Bedecked with ribbons that represents every theater of war. Who wore it last in our proud company? This full-dress uniform, W dash 2565, seen in Our Finest Hours, in Ruthless Combat, in Dogfights Over Broadway, and worn out finally, here on this spot, in Parallel Hell. What is it worth? How much do I hear?

ALVARADO [*off*]: That's metaphysically absurd, man! How could I know what you hear?

PICO: Yeah, fuck you!

KLEIN: I don't hear that!

LT TIREBITER: Five dollars!

KLEIN: I heard that! What do you think you're trying to do, Lieutenant? Buy your way out of these proceedings?

LT TIREBITER: I am out, Klein. I don't like you. I don't want a part in what you're selling. And I'm walking out of your set.

KLEIN: You can't do that!

LT TIREBITER: Watch me!

KLEIN: You'll never work in this town again, Tirebiter!

LT TIREBITER: What town?

SOUND: *Door slams.*

MAJOR: George, come back! Now, don't worry, Mr. Klein. Don't get mad. I'll bring him back. He's a good boy.

SOUND: *Door slams again. Courtroom crowd noises.*

DAD: A good boy gone bad! You move when you're told not to move. You take off your shoes to evade the men who are trying to protect you. You sneak into a forbidden sector after curfew, and you are caught with your hands up something they don't belong. My, my, my! Your friends at Commie Martyrs must be mighty proud of you.

PEORGIE: Dad, I don't have any friends at Commie Martyrs.

MUDHEAD: I've never even seen anyone from there!

PEORGIE: You're right, Mudhead. And no there's no room for anybody, 'cause it's all filled up with Morse Science.

MUDHEAD: Where'd they go?

PEORGIE: Yeah, where did all the kids go?

JUDGE: Well, they're in Korea.

PEORGIE & LT TIREBITER: On which side?

BAILIFF: Quiet, please, in the courtroom.

JUDGE: (What's that soldier doing in here?) What do you mean by that?

ALVARADO: What do you *mean* by that?

PICO: What do you mean by *that*?

SOUND: *Croud murmuring. Gavel pounds.*

LT TIREBITER: I mean, in whose movie?

JUDGE: This is no movie. This is real.

LT TIREBITER: Which reel?

JUDGE: The last reel of this vintage motion picture, "Highschool Madness." Lot Number M dash 25. Black and White. 35-millimeter . . .

PEORGIE: Oh, I see!

JUDGE: Now who started at five dollars?

PEORGIE: All right! I guess it was me!

LT TIREBITER: Nice goin', kid. See ya later.

JUDGE [*fading under*]: Let's go to 25. 25 bid, now 30, now 35. Thank you, sir. Go to 50. Go to a half $37.50, thank you sir . . .

PEORGIE [*to Mudhead*]: It's all a fake, Mudhead! They lied to me!

MUDHEAD: Who do you mean, "they"?

PEORGIE: You know, "Them."

MUDHEAD: Name three.

PEORGIE: Well, there's the Pooper, and . . .

MUDHEAD: You.

PEORGIE: And *me*!

MUDHEAD: Hey, whose movie is this?

PEORGIE: Yeah! It's nobody's now, Mudhead, 'cause I'm gettin' out!

MUDHEAD: How you gonna do it, Peorge?

JUDGE [*auctioneering*]: 50 bid. 55. 60. 75. A Hundred. First warning. One hundred dollars. Second warning. Third warning. Sold for a hundred dollars. A steal . . .

PEORGIE: I don't know.

MUDHEAD: How did you get in here?

PEORGIE: Oh, darn! I don't remember!

MUDHEAD: Well, where were you before?

PEORGIE: Before?

JUDGE [*continuing under*]: It's yours, sir. Easy 103. Here's another item. A lovely miniature executive in a brown tweed suit from a front room office . . .

MUDHEAD: Yeah!

PEORGIE: Right! I sold . . .

SOUND: *TV* Click!

DANNY DOLLAR: . . . Out! So here's your last deal, Mrs. Presky. Which would you rather do? Hit this Jew over the head with a bag of sugar or beat out that rhythm on a drum? Come on, love.

SOUND: *Shouts from audience.*

MRS PRESKY: I'll take the bag.

DANNY: You mean you're going to trade this four-foot cube of 18-carat Swiss bullion—and the snake knives, Mrs. Presky? All for that little bag?

MRS P: Yes! I want the bag!

DANNY: Well, all right, then. Open it up!

MRS P: Yes, yes! Uh—why—why this is a bag of shit!

DANNY: But it's really great shit, Mrs. Presky . . .

SOUND: *TV* Click!

BOB BASELINE: . . . on't spurt fire like the hoses. No, friends, this one won't take over the house like the high-speed vibrating clocks. So, friends, don't change . . .

SOUND: *TV* Click!

KATHY: More coffins, Warden?

WARDEN: I think I've seen enough!

KATHY: Then open up your cells and let go . . .

SOUND: *TV* Click!

ANNOUNCER 13: . . . Ed aims to please and so does Louise! So don't hide arms, get side arms, at Ames Guns! 30102 East Rhode Island School of Design Terrace in Yukaipah!

GIRL ANNOUNCER: Daddy, where can I get a good deal in a Christian atmosphere? . . .

SOUND: *TV* Click!

PASTOR FLASH: . . . ere, friends! Right here! God amighty, I'm full of it! But I'm going to let it go. And you've got to let it go. Dear Friends, just as sure as you can bet it, one of those two greatest guys up there is going to let go, just as you is letting go. Ahhhhhhhhhh . . . [*Fading to TV sound*] Isn't that great, my friends? Isn't that a load off your mind? I know it is off mine. Don't be afraid. Look at it! (Close the curtains, Fred.) Look at that steaming heap of plot-buttered goat custards! My, my . . .

SOUND: *TV is clicked off. A pause. The phone rings and is picked up.*

GEORGE: Hello?

OPERATOR: Good morning, Mr. Tirebiter. This is your service. Time to wake up.

GEORGE: Oh, that's all right, my dear. I've been up all night, watching myself on the TV.

OPERATOR: Oh . . .

GEORGE: I don't suppose there'd be any messages for me this morning?

OPERATOR: Just a moment. Yes, sir. There are some. A Mr. Sennett called . . .

GEORGE: Mr. Sennett?

OPERATOR: And a Mr. Keaton, Babe Hardy, Stan Jefferson, a Mr. Dunkerfield—oh—and Mr. Roach. Am I going too fast?

GEORGE: Mr. Roach? Oh, no, no. I'm remembering. I'm remembering them all. This is wonderful. Is there anyone else?

SOUND: *Ice cream truck bells in the distance.*

OPERATOR: There was a Mr. Turpin, a Mr. Fetchit. Oh, and a Mr. [*Honk*

Honk] He wouldn't leave his name. A Mr. Lloyd. A Charlie somebody . . .

GEORGE: Just a moment. I have to go get an ice cream cone. Hold on. I'll be right back . . .

OPERATOR: Mr. Tirebiter . . .

SOUND: *Bells approaching, running to door, door opening.*

GEORGE: I'm so hungry. Thank goodness you came up into the hills! Hey, hey! Wait for me! Hey, Mister! I got a nickel, wait for me . . .

SOUND: *Fading bells. Birds twittering, fading out.*

THE FIRESIGN THEATRE

I Think We're All Bozos On This Bus

If Bees Lived Inside Your Head

The five lifestyles of man in the future are, starting from top to bottom, though it's circular: First, The Berserker. Clue to a Berserker: Anybody who's got a gun. Anybody in a lime-green car with eight-foot tires, called Demon or Barracuda. Any Army officer, anybody in uniform. A Bobby is not a Berserker. But maybe he is because he carries his job, his badge. Most people who have jobs. There's a Berserker aspect to all of us. You can play softball with a Berserker. A Berserker doesn't always have to kill, but in the back of his mind, it's not a bad idea.

Under the Berserkers are the Zips. The archetypal Zip is the 1930s guy with the thin moustache. Zips have always been concerned with hair. We're exhibiting Zip tendencies in having rather fancily cut moustaches. We're all prone to these various aspects. There's a Zip in everyone's kip, is the World War One English expression. Zips love new products. Zips are often found inside new headphones. They've got zip, pep. Zzzzzip! Zip me up! Most actors are Zips. There's a category called Hip Zip, which David invented yesterday.

Bozo is the Brotherhood of Zips and Others. Bozos are people who band together for fun and profit. They have no jobs. Anybody who goes on a tour is a Bozo. Why does a Bozo cross the street? Because there's a Bozo on the other side. It comes from the phrase *vos otros*, meaning others. They're the huge, fat, middle waist. The archetype is an Irish drunk clown with red hair and nose, and pale skin. Fields, William Bendix. Everybody tends to drift toward Bozoness. It has Oz in it. They mean well. They're straight-looking except they've got inflatable shoes. They like their comforts. The Bozos have learned to enjoy their free time, which is all the time.

Now, the Boogies. You see a bunch of Boogies around you. That's our lifestyle. There are more spades in this class than any other. But the world is changing. There are now getting to be a lot of spade Zips. And spade Bozos. Boogies don't differentiate between grass and alchohol. People who work in post offices are generally Boogies. They take it easy. They don't Zip. They're not Bozos because they don't clone. They boogie around rather than hanging around one another. They Boogie.

The other class is the Beaners. The Beaners live outside the Law of Gravity. They have more color television sets than anybody in the world. They're always appearing either on or with your color TV. They watch themselves on color TV. Beaners are very concerned with their own refuse, which they leave piled up around their house, but always in use. They're always going to use it. Hundreds of old pickup trucks. All Indians are Beaners. They don't care. Why should they? Beaners can't tell lies. They fear no one. "Don't point your finger at me, Daddy-o, I cut it off!" Pico and Alvarado are Beaners. We love the Beaners.

Most youth is Bozo-like now. That's why people get so upset when Berserkers come into a Bozo gathering. 'Cause Bozos never do anything to any-

body. Bozos keep having rock festivals. They create marijuana free-areas. Grass has moved into Bozodom.

The Berserkers and Zips run things now. Why does a Zip pay taxes? Because he likes to fill out the forms. Berserkers run things by telling you the Beaners are going to get you. Those desperate Beaners may strike at any time! All politicians are Berserkers. ·

Intrat Et Exit Ut Nil Supra!

We had often talked about writing a children's record. Sometimes the talk concerned a record *for* children, but more often it was the *form* of a children's album which appealed to us. Before the writing of *Dwarf*, we had discussed an album featuring a character called St. Beepo, The Macrocephalic Clown—an obvious ancestor of Barney Bozo. During September and October, 1970, we had written a couple of false starts for an album to be titled "Why Does The Porridge Bird Lay Its Eggs In The Air?" which starred various animal characters. Even earlier, we had outlined a kid's radio program called "The Whisperin' Squash Show," with a story-teller named Dr. Memory and an all-vegetable cast of cowboys and badmen.

When we started writing *Bozos* on April 15th, 1971, the manuscript was titled "Biting Through," after the hexagram we had thrown twice—once on the final day of *Dwarf*, and again as we began work on the fourth album. Indeed, our character did seem to have "bitten through"—to have escaped into a world over which he could exercise some measure of personal control. Once again, we began by turning on the electricity. In this case, it was the electric typewriter which sat ready on the round table. The writing proceeded, serial-fashion, until the 23rd of June, interrupted by sessions in the studio in which we recorded what had been written to date. Always, the next episode in the story was unclear to us until the previous episode had been completely produced. The plot unwound as slowly as a mystery novel.

Bozos begins on the same street down which George Tirebiter had just pursued the ice-cream truck. Hunger satisfied, and with nothing else to do on a beautiful Fall morning, George—now transmogrified into a young man named Clem—is amused and intrigued by the arrival of the Future Fair Tour Bus. He watches familiar cartoon characters invite him electronically aboard and, shoeless and care-free, decides to join the Bozos.

Inside the Bus, surrounded by an ever-changing synthetic environment, Clem and his seat-mate Barney are kept entertained by the electronic system which guides the Bus and the Fair itself.

Clem, not used to Bozoing about, leaves Barney and decides to take a ride through one of the Fair's main shows, The Wall Of Science. The Wall submerges its viewers into an animated, multi-dimensional educational exhibit, in which they are treated to a History of Life, from Before the Beginning, on through the Dawn of Man, The Age of Enlightenment and finally The Scientific Era.

At last, the Wall arrives at The Future itself. Government representatives now present Clem and the rest of the audience a dramatized lecture on the System, in order to prepare them for the Fair's biggest attraction, a personal visit with The President.

Each Fair-goer is treated to this realistic scene in turn, and in each case The President speaks directly to the individual, attempting to answer each personal question. It is at this point that Clem, for reasons of his own, reprograms the system which controls the operation of the Fair and its many elements. He reaches deeply into the core of the system, but is unable to find the program which will answer the question he poses: "Why does the porridge bird lay his egg in the air?" In self-defense, the system shuts down The President and shunts off the audience to the Funway—a vast arena filled with noisy, diverting entertainments and crowds of gawking Bozos.

Clem, concerned that his connection with the broken ride will get him into trouble, joins Barney in an attempt to lose himself in the crowd. But, before they can get on one of the amusement cars, he is identified by one of the Fair's holographic sentinels. Fortunately, Clem knows enough to un-program the hologram of Artie Choke, and to re-program it in his own likeness. So doing, he creates his electronic double and sends it back into the system itself, where it searches through the machine's storage units to find the central memory core. The system resists the unauthorized (gypsy) program as best it can, but must finally check it out with the deepest cybernetic unit of all, the binomial duality known as Dr. Memory.

Clem's desperate program asks of Dr. Memory an unanswerable question. Confused, the Doctor is vulnerable and turns the entire machine off at its source. The Fair and all its creations vanish, leaving only the fireworks of its departure.

And now, the story changes. The Future is Past. And whose Future was it, anyhow? We leave you to ponder this question, even as we are pondering it ourselves.

Shhhhhhhh! Quiet now! here comes that little sailor . . .

Hideo Gump Sr.

Toyko, 1972

I Think We're All Bozos On This Bus

SOUNDS: *Typewriter click on and hum. Wind. Birds chirrupping. Ducks. Ice-cream truck bells fading away.*

PUBLIC ADDRESS VOICE [*fading on*]: . . . Biting Through in this Area, and it's just starting now.

SOUNDS: *Wind blowing leaves. Someone walking down the street, whistling. Music on a Sound Truck, getting closer.*

PA VOICE [*Moving closer*]: Live in the Future! Yes, live in the Future, now! It's right around the corner. Yes, in fact, it's come right here to beautiful *THIS AREA**!

CLEM: What's that?

PA VOICE: The Future Fair! A Fair for All, and no fare to anybody! Yes, it's free! Join the expectant crowd gathering now, as we stop here on DUTCH ELM STREET* . . .

CLEM: Holy Fudd!

PA VOICE: Come closer, folks. Don't crowd the wheels . . .

SOUND: *The Future Fair Bus stops. A hologram appears like a bursting bubble.*

THE WHISPERIN' SQUASH [*singing*]:
> Back from the shadows again!
> Out where an In-jun's your friend!
> Where the veg'tables are green,
> And you can pee into the stream!
> Yes, we're back from the Shadows again!

WHISPERIN': Howdy, everybody! Ah'm the Whisperin' Squash . . .

LONESOME: And I'm the Lonesome Beet . . .

ARTIE: And I'm Artie Choke! And we're just a joke . . .

WHISPERIN': And don't be afraid, Little People, 'cause we're just Holy-grams!

CLEM [*aside*]: Great!

LONESOME: Yeah! But what about you, Pardner? What'ch you doin' today?

ARTIE: Can't be much, Lonesome. Nobody's workin'!

LONESOME: Nobody 'cept us and I'm gettin' tired of standin' here with these geeks a-gawkin' at me!

ARTIE: Now you keep it sweet, Beet!

LONESOME: Listen here, Leafhead! I'm gonna pluck you five ways . . .

WHISPERIN': Now, now, boys! Fightin's out of style! Fun's where the Fair's at—in the Future, that is!

ARTIE: You can bet your roots, Toots, it's Tons o' Fun!

LONESOME: And technical stimulation!

---

*Indicates a taped insert by another announcer's voice.

CLEM [*aside*]: That's what I need!

WHISPERIN': And there's lots more of *me* where I come from!

LONESOME: In Gov'ment inflicted simulation!

ARTIE: The Future can't wait—no place to hide!

LONESOME: Yep! So climb on a board . . .

ARTIE: We're goin' inside!

WHISPERIN' [*singing, with the others*]:
>   We're goin' back to the Shadows again!
>   Out where an Indian's your friend!
>   Where the vegetables are green,
>   And you can pee right into the stream!
>   (And that's important!)
>   We're back from the Shadows again!

PA VOICE: Doors Open!

SOUND: *The Holograms disappear.*

PA VOICE: Doors close in five seconds.

CLEM: Pluck the Duck! Who have I got to lose?

SOUNDS: *Music over the PA changes perspective as* CLEM *climbs aboard.*

PA VOICE: Live in the Future! It's just starting now . . .

SOUNDS: *Bus doors close, cutting off* VOICE. *People talking.*

MICKEY [*automated hostess*]: Welcome in. Now, follow the rubber line to your seat.

CLEM: Oh. . . . Say, excuse me, is this window taken?

BARNEY: Ah, no. Certainly—no, no! Take your seat.

CLEM: Thank you.

SOUND: CLEM *sits down with a loud squishing noise.*

BARNEY: Say, it's soft, isn't it?

CLEM: That's really comfortable. Just like sitting in a big hand . . .

MICKEY: Comfy? Now, here's famous broadcaster Floyd Damme.

FLOYD: Hello, Globetrotters! While we're still on the ground, let's look around and see where we are . . .

SOUND: *Big reaction from the Bozos on the Bus.*

FLOYD: In the windows to your left, it's five thousand feet to the bottom of the Grand Canyo-ooo-ooo-on . . .

SOUND: *The Bozos react to the simulated view and music underscore.*

FLOYD: Yet now, as inevitable as dawn, the Sun, arching on its axis, rises to meet the East—chariot-racing across the high noon desert sky, only to plummit, like bald Icarus, into the sensual, fermenting seas of the South Pacific. And even now, yet, as scary night descends upon us, we could appreciate the Wonders of Nature as stimulating as Man's Own Triumphs! Let us pause . . .

SOUNDS: *Applause and approval from the Bozos.*

CLEM: Incredible illusion!

MICKEY: That was our final groundstop. Ladies and gentlemen, children, Bozos, we are now in lift mode.

BARNEY [*close perspective, over Mickey*]: Uh—say, I'm a Bozo!

CLEM: I thought you had kind of a big nose.

BARNEY: You recognized it, huh?

CLEM: Yeah.

BARNEY: You like to give it a squeeze?

CLEM: Oh, no . . .

BARNEY: Go on, squeeze the wheeze! Many people like to.

SOUND: *Loud Honk!*

BARNEY: See? It doesn't hurt me.

CLEM: No . . .

BARNEY: You know, I think we're all Bozos on this bus!

SOUND: BARNEY *honks his nose and there is a chorus of honks in reply.*

CLEM: My mother was a Bozo-ette at school.

BARNEY: No kidding! You know, my Ma always said, "You gotta start young if you're gonna stick it out!"

CLEM: Well, my mother didn't talk to me much . . .

BARNEY: Poor kid!

MICKEY: Now, please, everyone lock your wigs, let the air out of your shoes and prepare yourselves for a period of simulated exhilaration. Everybody ready? Let's get in "sync" for our Flight To The Future!

CLEM [*sync-ing with Mickey*]: Excuse me, I'm just going to "sync" in . . .

BARNEY: Not too far there . . .

SOUNDS: *Simulated jet takeoffs and echo-effects.*

PA VOICES: The Future is Fun! The Future is Fair! You may already have won! You may already be there!

SOUND: *Musical fanfare.*

PA VOICES: Hello! We're glad you made it! Welcome to The Future!

SOUND: *Jet fly-bys and applause. The music and carnival sound of the Fair fades up.*

BARNEY: Was that simulated, do ya suppose?

CLEM: Who knows?

MICKEY: We are docked and open. Be sure to inflate shoes before crossing the water. Remember, the Rubber Lines are for your convenience and protection. Thank you . . . [*Repeats under*]

BARNEY: Oh, well. Hey! Don't forget to pump your shoes!

CLEM: I don't wear 'em any more. I gave 'em up years ago.

BARNEY: Oh. Well . . . come on.

SOUNDS: *Passengers debarking from The Bus and entering Fair.*

PA ANNOUNCERETTE: All Bozos and Bozo-ettes, please clone under the Big Blue

Thank you.

BARNEY: Well, I must go where the Bozos go, kid.

CLEM: Yeah, I'll bet. So long.

BARNEY: Yeah, the longer the better!

CLEM: Honk, honk!

BARNEY: Now, listen, kid—I'm alone, I got to clone. Maybe we'll run into each other on the Funway, huh?

A BOZO [*calling*]: Hey, Barney! Chairman Barney!

CLEM: Yeah, you bet, Honky. Honk, honk! [*Sighs*]

SOUND: *Hologram popping up, music playing.*

LONESOME: He, he! Howdy, little Pardner! Well, which way ya goin' now?

CLEM: I don't know, Mr. Beet.

LONESOME: Yep! That's right! Ya could cut 'em off at the Past!

CLEM: What?

LONESOME: But I'd like to recommend WALL OF SCIENCE, 'cause it's my favorite! Jest climb aboard that old YELLOW rubber line. Well, thankya, Pardner. See ya on the Funway! Yippee! Tie one on! So long . . .

SOUND: *The hologram disappears.*

CLEM: So long, Beethead! Give my . . . I'm standing here like an idiot talkin' to myself . . . I might as well walk over to the old yellow line and stand here on the yellow line like an idiot talkin' to myself . . .

SOUND: *The rubber line humming.*

VOICE OF THE LINE: You have chosen The Path Of Science. Stand in the middle of rubber line.

CLEM: That's where I am. Real comfy . . .

VOICE OF THE LINE: Please keep your hands to yourself. Thank you.

CLEM: You're welcome . . . It's moving right along . . .

SOUNDS: *The line merges with a rolling of thunder. Wolves howl.*

VOICE OF GOD: Before the Beginning, there was this Turtle. And the Turtle was alone. And he looked around, and he saw his neighbor, which was his Mother. And he lay down on top of his neighbor, and behold, she bore him in tears, an oak tree. Which grew all day, and then fell over, like a bridge. And lo, under the bridge there came a Catfish, and he was very big, and he was walking, and he was the biggest he had seen. [*Fading*] And so were the firey balls of this fish, one of which is the Sun, and the other, they called the Moon . . .

EXPERT VOICE: Yes, some uncomplicated peoples still believe this myth. But here, in the technical vastness of the Future, we can guess that surely the Past was very different. We can surmise, for instance, that these two great balls . . . [*Cross fading*]

DR TECHNICAL [*fading up*]: We know for certain, for instance, that for some

reason, for some time in the beginning, there were hot lumps. Cold and lonely, they whirled noiselessly through the black holes of space. These insignificant lumps came together to form the first union—our Sun, the heating system. And about this glowing gasbag rotated the Earth, a cat's-eye among aggies, blinking in astonishment across the Face of Time . . .

STUDENT: Well, we were covered with a molten scum of rocks, bobbing on the surface like rats. Later, when there was less heat, these giant rock-groups settled down among the land masses. During this extinct time, our Earth was like a steam room, and no one, not even Man, could get in. However, the oceans and the sewers were simmering with a rich protein stew, and the mountains moved in to surround and protect them. They didn't know then that living as we know it was already taken over . . .

SOUND: *Applause and snickering.*

GRAD STUDENT: Animals without backbones hid from each other, or fell down. Clamasaurs and oysterettes appeared as appetizers. Then came the sponges, which sucked up about ten percent of all life. Hundreds of years later, in the Late Devouring Period, fish became obnoxious. Trailerbikes, chiggerbites and mosquitoes collided aimlessly in the dense gas. Finally, tiny edible plants sprang up in rows, giving birth to generations of insecticides and other small, dying creatures. Thank you.

SOUND: *Applause and a roll of thunder. Primitive music.*

VOICE OF GOD: Millions of months passed, and twenty-eight days later, the moon appeared. This small change was reflected best, perhaps, in the Sand-dollar, which shrank to almost nothing at the bottom of the pool. Where even dumb amphibians like Catfish laid their eggs in the boiling waters, only to be gobbled up every three minutes by the giant Sea-Orphans and Jungle Bunnies, which scared everybody. And so, in fear and hot water, Man is born!

SOUND: *Another roll of thunder. Animals howling.*

FIRST MAN: I am La Brea Man. I am First Man. Wife and I live in pits. I discover pain and boredom and how to use hands in self-defense . . .

SECOND MAN: I am his son. I am called Plowman. I was the first to dig the earth, and make the rivers run backward. There was no stopping me—or my wife!

FOUR MEN: I am his many cousins. I chip the stone. I smelt the rock. I bronzed the shoe. I lay the asphalt. Together we made enough noise to keep the wolves awake!

ENGLISHMAN: I am his Godson—Sybilized Man. I harnessed the secret of the calendar, and with the power of the week, I built the pyramids.

OLD MAN: I am his Mentor—Hippocrices. I put him through school, where he learned to stand up for a principal, and sit down on his own stool.

LAST MAN: I am his father, Cesarian. I sent him away from home for something to live on, and paid him to fight over it!

112

SOUNDS: *Battle noises fading.*

EXPERT VOICE: So now, everywhere he went, Man dropped a great load of knowledge, forming a rich compost where slumbered the modifying spark of Humanity. Yet, it was not many years later, in the little Phlegmish village of Gotterdam, that the restless chemist Sir Sydney Fudd was to make that particularly momentous entry in his scientific journal . . . [*cross fades*]

FUDD [*fading up*]: . . . love you! You obt. svt., "Fuddles." That ought to do it. [*Reading back*] Dear Nabby . . . [*Corrects letter*] Darling Nabby . . . Thanks for the pomegranates, Spunky loves them, and will be sitting up soon, I hope. As for the excellent porcelain astrolab . . . "a"? There's an "e" in there—"astrolabe" . . . which miraculously arrived in precise working condition after its perilous journey 'round the Tit—oh, Tip—oh dear, that's a "p"—"Tip" . . . I set it up directly, and having once aligned it upon the Celestial Doggie, the sight so roused me, that I was seized by a transport of scientific rapture! And, whilst a happy prisoner of this unhappy state, I fell upon my glorious machine, and knocked it, perforce, up—down—the kitchen stairs, carrying faithful Bunky—Spunky—with it. You can imagine my confusion. But, *quid malmborg in plano*, consternation turned to lucidation. (Period there.) Could this be the solution to our problems, both personal and scientifick? Howsoever, a devilishly natural principal of science had revealed itself—exclamation point—and, through my quivering quill, I present it to you thus—quote—"If you push something hard enough, it will fall over." End quote. So little did this console poor Spunky, that I was compelled [*Fading*] to lie on her for at least a fortnight . . .

SOUND: *Loud ding.*

NARRATOR: "If you push something hard enough, it will fall over!" Fudd's First Law of Opposition. How can we best illustrate the stubborn consistency of this eternal principle? . . .

SOUNDS: *Birds singing. Feet on snow.*

NARRATOR: By walking down this shady New England lane on Wednesday, 1875. We pause before the grounded iron gate of Dr. Beddoe's Pneumatic Institute, and eavesdrop upon two members of the Amateur Electrical League . . .

SOUND: *The Machine wheezing and pumping.*

TOM: Dick! Dick! She works!

DICK: It does, it does, Tom! It comes in and goes out like anything!

TOM: And to think all I had to do was put the balls on the other side!

DICK: Look at 'em spin now!

TOM: Aren't they beautiful!

DICK: Oh, Tom, Tom! Those balls will mean your fortune!

TOM: By Fudd! I'll patent this machine, and name it after Nancy!

DICK: What? You mean Pushover?

TOM: Yes, because that's what she does. And she'll run everything!

DICK: Everywhere!

TOM: Every time!

DICK: For ever!

TOM: For everybody! . . .

SOUND: *Another loud ding.*

NARRATOR: "It comes in, it must go out." Teslacle's Deviant to Fudd's Law. So, with the invention of the Motor Operated Pushover, Man and Science gave birth to life here, today, in the Future! Man, woman, child! All is up against the Wall Of Science!

SOUND: *Musical fanfare.*

WELTER OF "REAL" VOICES:

> I like the future—I'm in it!
> Built it myself, and I love it!
> I'm not sure . . .
> Personally, I'm very pleased.
> No, I think it's going to be all right.
> I can dig it.
> How do I like the Future? Well, the Future's not here yet, man!
> Smaller, but cleaner.
> Right on!
> I say live it or live with it!
> Straight ahead!
> Well, I think it has quite a great future in it. It's electric.

SOUND: *Zap of electricity.*

CHESTER: This is the Honorable Chester Cadaver. Sure, understanding today's complex world of the Future is a little like having bees live in your head. But—there they are! And, like the young lady said . . .

LADY: I say live it, or live with it!!

CHESTER: What does this mean? Well, for the straight poop, let's go where I go every morning. Centrally located and barely a strone's throw from the Tomb of the Unregistered Voter, downstairs in the historic Old Grid Building . . . [*crossfading to a new location*] Hello, Clive!

MR BROWN: Come in, Chester!

CHESTER: Thank you!

MR BROWN: Hey, hey! You're just in time to help me check out this new Model Government. They just brought it down, and they say it explains everything.

CHESTER: Well, you know, it sure is big!

MR BROWN: Look, look over there in the Left End. That's where you work, there, in the Bureau of Western Mythology . . .

CHESTER: By golly! We're a proud service of the Lost Electricity Reclamation

MR BROWN: Yeah, the L.E.S. is under the Left . . . uh . . .

CHESTER: I don't . . .

MR BROWN: I think I'll just plug it in . . .

CHESTER: Oh, listen, I'll just use this little plug right down here.

MR BROWN: Achtung! Not that plug, Chucko! Uh-uhm! See . . .

SOUND: *Zap of electricity.*

CHESTER: Oh! That's terrible!

MR BROWN: You gotta plug in the female!

SOUND: *The Machine working.*

MR BROWN: Ah! Listen to it. Teaches ya, huh? "Half a watt comes in here . . ."

CHESTER: ". . . Must go out there!"

MR BROWN: Right-O! Let's see what it does with this fine miniature boxcar of industrial coke. Let's lock and load here . . .

CHESTER: Oh, yeah! Look at that! That's amazing!

MR BROWN: Let's see . . . pumped from the Veteran's Tap-Dance Administration . . .

CHESTER: And it goes up here to the Assistant Secretary of Left-Overs . . .

MR BROWN: Flip-flop down to the Secretary of Covers . . .

CHESTER: Watch it go now! Around the Department of Spies . . .

MR BROWN: And into the office of the Secretary of Failure, himself. Wouldn't you know? That's Shoes For Industry, Charlie.

CHESTER: And it's food for thought, you know, Mr. Brown.

MR BROWN: Yeah. But we're thinking about Power, Chucko.

CHESTER: Well, I know you are, or you wouldn't be here.

SOUND: *A new noise from the Machine.*

MR BROWN: Oh! Look at that, Herb! It heard the word Power, and it responded, just like we do . . . and here it comes . . . Here comes our ox-cart, right back to Earth, smack-dab on the middle of the Small Animal Administration!

CHESTER: Well, I must say—that's the most incredible demonstration . . . but where are the Humans, Officer?

MR BROWN: Why, they're right here, son. Waiting in the lobby to use the power of that ton of coke.

CHESTER: Oh! Then we must be very near the President, Mr. Dithers?

MR BROWN: Yes, Dagwood. He's the Terminal Buss. The output.

CHESTER: I'll betcha he really puts out!

MR BROWN: That's right! Everyone's always asking him questions.

CHESTER: Oh, well, maybe my friend would like to ask something. He's been with us since before the Beginning, sir. He must be bursting with a short question about his place in the Future.

MR BROWN: Oh, is he your friend?

CHESTER: Yes.

MR BROWN: Well, ask him his name.

CHESTER: Oh, I'm sorry. Could you state your name? [*Long pause*] Please state your name.

CLEM [*after a pause*]: Oh, do you want me to . . .

CHESTER: Please state your first name.

CLEM: Uh—Clem . . .

CHESTER: Thank you, [UHCLEM].* Now we can introduce you, and some of your selected neighbors, to our President.

CLEM: Thanks . . .

VOICE OF THE LINE: Step off stopping yellow line.

CLEM: OK.

VOICE OF THE LINE: Stand on steady blue line.

CLEM: It's throbbing . . .

VOICE OF THE LINE: You are now going to see the President. No flashes please. Thank you.

CLEM: Ready or not, Springhead, here I come!

SOUND: *The line disappearing on to the other side.*

[End of Side One.]

SOUND: *Fanfare.*

GUIDE: Mr. President, I'd like to introduce you to [JIM].

JIM: Hiya, Mr. President!

PRES: Hello. Always nice to see you, [JIM]. You know, the mainspring of this country, wound up as tight as it is, is guaranteed for the life of the watch. And who's watching? People like you, [JIM], and you, [BARNEY]. People who are alerted and unafraid to waste the little time that I've scheduled just for your question. State short question.

JIM: Well, Mr. President. It's the bees 'n' spiders again! They stole my food stamps, and sold 'em to the rats, an' I tried to get down to my car fo' to honk the horn for he'p, but the snakes is guardin' it for the cock-aroaches! I go back upstairs, but the spiders is jammed the police-lock. I ain't been inside fo' a week! And I know that my wife is sleepin' wif the bees . . .

PRES: Could you state that as a question, please?

JIM: Well, sure, Mr. President. Where can I get a job?

PRES: M-Many busy executives ask me, "What about the Job Displacement Market Program in the City of the Future?" Well, count on *us* to be

*Clem's own voice on tape.

there, [JIM]. Because, if we're lucky tomorrow, we won't have to deal with questions like yours ever again.

SOUND: *Applause.*

JIM: Oh, that Springhead! The rats told me he ain't goin' to be straight with me . . . [*fading*]

SOUND: *Fanfare.*

GUIDE: Thank you for the question. Exit left to Funway. Mr. President, I'd like to introduce you to [BARNEY].

PRES: Hello. Always glad to talk to you, [BARNEY]. You know, when you clock the human race with the stopwatch of History, it's a new record every time. And who wins? And who loses? People like you, [BARNEY], and you, [UHCLEM]. People who are altered . . .

BARNEY: Stop! Stop, Mr. President! Please stop! Now, I know it means nothing to you. I'm only a clone. But you've got such a wonderful job, and you're doing it so well! Ya know, we Bozos have a saying: "When ya put on the nose, it grow . . .!"

PRES: Could you state that as a questio . . .[READ TO] . . . Thank you very much, [BARNEY]. You'll be getting a handsome simulfax copy of your own words in the mail soon. And my reply.

BARNEY: Oh! By golly, Mr. President, you're beneficent . . .

SOUND: *Applause.*

GUIDE: Thank you for question. Exit right to Funway.

SOUND: *Fanfare.*

GUIDE: Mr. President, I'd like to introduce you to [UHCLEM].

PRES: Hello. Always nice to see you, [UHCLEM]. You know, the springhead of this country . . .

CLEM: Alright, stop, Mr. President. Mr. President, stop, please! Now listen to me. This is Worker speaking. Hello.

PRES: Hello. How are ya'? State maintenance question.

CLEM: Fine, thanks. No, no. Read me Dr. Memory.

PRES: AMRAD . . . It's not sure I understand you fully. Could you state that as a question, please?

CLEM: Read me Dr. Memory?

PRES: SYSTAT. DIRECT READOUT. UPTIME 9:01 . . .

BEANER [*waiting in line*]: Hey, man! Ask him a question!

CLEM: Shhh!

PRES: I have been awake for 9 hours, 1 minute, 44 seconds. AMYL FAX SHUFFLE TIME. Less than 1 percent of freight drain, LOG FIVE. 5 jobs, 2 detached. MINIMUM ENTRY. GATE ONE . . .

BEANER: Hijolé, man! This is so boring!

PRES: Totalling balance National Debt—3-4-5-6 boxcars. GATE CLOSED.

CLEM: OK! Alright, you're doing fine, but this is a Flip-Flop, Springhead.

CLEM: I'm gonna ask you a question that you won't be able to answer.

PRES: I am not sure I understand you fully. LOG OUT. RUN OFF. MEMO-RY. A.—"The system is less energetic if domains of opposite directions alternate." NPN READ MACNAM. PNP READ MACNAM . . .

BEANER: What is he talkin' about?

PRES: PASSWORD. Maximum Output Resource Yield. ILLEGAL ENTRY. Try again.

CLEM: Yes, we're going to try again. Open your Gate, Doctor.

PRES: SIS, PUP . . .

CLEM: That's right!

PRES: DAD, BUB, MOM, PIP, DAD, DUD . . .

CLEM: It's repeating . . .

BEANER: He's got little squinty eyes, though . . .

PRES: DID, MOM, MEM, MIM, MOM, MEM . . .

CLEM: Mem . . .

PRES: MEM . . .

CLEM: Mem . . .

PRES: MEM, MEM, MEM, MEM . . .

CLEM: Memory!

PRES: Direct readout. Dr. Memory, [UHCLEM].

CLEM: Thank you, thank you. Now, Doctor—I'm speaking to you, Doctor . . .

DR M: MMMMMMMMMM?

CLEM: Something the leprechauns asked me when I was a sprout in Indiana has always puzzled me. Doctor? Question. Evaluate. Why does the porridge bird lay his egg in the air?

BEANER: What's he talkin' about?

PAOLO: What's going on in there?

BEANER: I don't know, man . . .

PRES: LAUGH. RUNAWAY. The Doctor makes no readout. Read UN-HAPPY MACNAM. UNHAPPY MACNAM. SYSTAT. UPTIME 9:01. I have been awake for 9 hours, 2 minutes, 36 seconds . . .

BEANER: I think he broke it!

PAOLO: Yo no puedo . . .

PRES: . . . et . . . ek . . . [*voice breaks, doubles up*] . . . And I'm as tired of it as you are. And I hope that our children will come to love us again in some better world than this . . .

BEANER: I don' know—I think he's going to break it . . .

CLEM: Oh, Damn!

SOUND: *Applause.*

GUIDE: Thank you for question. Exit center to Funway.

BEANER: OK, it's me now, huh? What did you do to him?

GUIDE: Mr. President, I'd like to introduce you to [UHCLEM].

BEANER: No, man! No! It's not Clem, man!

PRES: Illegal character in line. RUB OUT. Go away.

BEANER: What's happening?

CLEM: Just a second, will ya please?

PRES: I'm sorry, this ride is closed.

BEANER: This ride is closed!?

GUIDE: Exit center to Fu . . . uh . . . err . . . [*Breaks down*]

BEANER: I been waiting for ten minutes from here to listen to the President
talk to me! What's happening? I think he broke . . . hey, Paolo! He
broke the President!

PAOLO: I'm gonna get my wife!

BEANER: It's all smashed in there . . .

SOUND: *The Funway sounds drown out the Beaner.*

BARNEY [*calling*]: Hey! Hey, kid! Come over here! Hey! How ya doin'! President gonna give ya a new pair of shoes?

CLEM: He's working on it. Hey, Barney, listen . . .

BARNEY: You know, a fine looking kind of man, I thought. Real regular features. Real regular clothes.

CLEM: Yeah, very incredible illusion. Very real.

BARNEY: Hey, what are you going to do next, kid . . .

CLEM [*on top*]: What are you gonna do next . . . Isn't that funny? I just came
over to ask you the same question.

BARNEY: Gosh! You have some free time . . .

CLEM: I wish I had nothing but free time.

BARNEY: Where's the schedule here? The future schedule? . . .

SOUTHERN ANNOUNCERETTE ON PA: Will our Guest Mr. Ahclem please drop by
the Hospitality Tower immediately? Thank you.

BARNEY: Oh my gosh! Now, this is one I've been waiting for! Look at this!
Malmborg In Plano! A Below-The-Belt, Bottoms-Out Revue! [*Laughs*]
Oh! It's not till tonight . . .

CLEM: Well, let's just walk around the Funway for a little while. What do you
say?

BARNEY: Oh, Kid, you're Hip like a Zip. Let's take a trip.

CLEM: Great! Let's just walk across the tracks . . .

LATIN ANNOUNCERETTE ON PA: Will our guest Mr. Ahclem report to the Hospitality Shelter in his Area? Thank you.

BARNEY: This fella Ah Clem's pretty popular . . .

CLEM: Yeah . . .

BARNEY: We could take one of these Big Red Cars that'll come along here.

Hey! Here's a cute story.

CLEM: What?

BARNEY: Why does a Bozo cross the road?

CLEM: What are you talking about?

BARNEY: 'Cause there's a Bozo on the other side!

CLEM: I see. That's very logical.

BARNEY: OK. Why does a Short-Hair cross the road?

CLEM: Uh . . . I don't know.

BARNEY: Because someone told him to!

CLEM: Oh, I see.

BARNEY: OK, now—why does a Long-Hair cross the road?

CLEM: Because someone told him not to?

BARNEY: Oh. Oh, well, you knew that one . . . well . . . Here comes a car . . .

MARK TIME [*approaching*]: . . . You'll thrill with your friends and family as you ride with Salamander Mark Time and my anxious android Chucko, the Rocket Robot, through the Black Hole of Space!

CHUCKO: Mark! Mark! Mark! They're performing experiments on animals in space! Mark! Mark! Mark! They're performing horrible . . . [*Kick!*] Thank you . . .

MARK TIME: Yes, this is going to be another exciting mission, Chucko. We'll be going to the Haunted Space Station for further instructions!

CHUCKO: You'll need a crowbar . . . [*Kick!*] A crew, Mark!

MARK: Right! I need some brave boys and girls who aren't afraid to live outside the Law of Gravity. Families who like to sleep in tubes and push buttons. Adventurers like you . . .

CHUCKO: All schlep inside for Mark Time's Outlaw Ghost Ship and further information, now boring . . . [*Kick!*] Boarding! Thank you . . .

MARK TIME [*fading off*]: You'll thrill with your friends and family as you ride with Salamander Mark Time and my . . .

CLEM: Let's go! Let's get on that one!

BARNEY: Naw! No, no, kid. That's for Beaners. You know—Boogies—people who like to be alone. I got to clone, kid. Don't worry, look—here comes another one—"just like the other one!"

PITCHMAN [*approaching fast*]: Swerve 'em!

GIRL: Dodge 'em!

PITCHMAN: Trick 'em!

GIRL: Push 'em over!

PITCHMAN: Tell 'em lies!

GIRL: Here's where Robot's Rules of Order don't apply! At Hideo Knutt's Boltadrome!

PITCHMAN: As seen on Who Asked For It! Strap on the Servo-Mitts and pit your metal against common household appliances!

GIRL: Step right up, sailor!

CLEM: Let's go!

PITCHMAN: Think you could go three rounds with this water heater, sailor? Looks easy, but sealed to the back of this metal mother is a radar-activated stamping and seizing module that'll keep a man punching 'till he's drunk with power! A man like you! . . .

GIRL: All up inside for Hideo Knutt's Boltadrome!

PITCHMAN: And further reclamation! Thank you . . .

SOUND: *Boltadrome fading off.*

CLEM: Come on, Barney! We can take on a couple of toasters or something . . .

BARNEY: Now, look, Kid. I drempt I went there once, but fightin's out of style now . . .

CLEM: Well, I'm gonna take the next car no matter what. OK?

SOUND: *Hologram appearing. Music.*

ARTIE: Ha, ha, Hi! Little parner! My name's Artie! Say, ya know I could tell just by listening that your name is [UHCLEM] and say, your poor Mommy or Daddy is waiting for you at the Hospitality Shelter. You better rustle your leaves over there!

BARNEY: Ah! This is exciting! Is your Mommy or Daddy waiting for you?

CLEM: Oh, come on now. They've just got me confused with someone. My parents . . .

ARTIE: Ah! Don't be afraid. I know it's you. Guess what? I'll race you there. Now, Artie can travel by the speed of light, but if you stand on that candy-stripe line right now, I bet you half-a-beet you'll beat me. Ready, step, go! . . .

BARNEY: Go! Well, now, maybe your Mother does want to talk to you, Kid! You know, "you just can't forget that sweet Bozoette . . ."!

CLEM: Barney, this is just a computer . . .

BARNEY: What? . . .

ARTIE: Oh, I see! You're too frightened or tired to move. Well, just stand there and I'll send Deputy Dan to get you.

BARNEY: That's right! Deputy Dan will find us! It'll be OK.

CLEM: Oh, no!

ARTIE: I'll wait here and kinda watch you 'till Dan comes . . .

CLEM: Let's go back into the Wall . . . This is stu . . . All right, listen, Chokehead. This is Worker speaking. Hello.

ARTIE: Hi! Open for maintenance alignment.

BARNEY: What have you done?

CLEM: Good! Now, let me show you something, Bozo! Detail dress circuits.

ARTIE: Belt. Above "A." Below "B."

CLEM: OK. Close "B" clothes mode.

BARNEY: Oh, my Duck! His pants have disappeared! Kid, everybody's watchin' . . .

Watch Them LAUGH As they come OUT !

CLEM: Come on now. Watch this! Ego . . .

ARTIE: Go . . .

CLEM: Close Artichoke mode.

SOUND: *Formless hologram humming.*

BARNEY: It's a rainbow! Now, what happened to little Artie?

CLEM: Prepare, shift, simulfax for hue and form. Prepare for mirror clone . . .

BARNEY: What are you doing?

CLEM: Clone me!

MAC: Password. Illegal entry.

CLEM: Clone *me*, Dr. Memory?

MAC: Thank you.

SOUND: *Hologram cloning.*

CLEM/CLONE: Hello. I'm Uhclem.

BARNEY: It's you!

CLEM: No, Barney! I'm me. That's just a hologram.

BARNEY: Well, Kid, you're a wizard whoever you are!

CLEM: No, I'm just trying to get a straight answer to something.

CLEM/CLONE: You have violated Robot's Rules of Order, and will be asked to leave the Future immediately. Thank you.

CLEM: Now, you can't talk to me like that! I demand to see Dr. Memory!

BARNEY: Hey! Here comes Deputy Dan!

CLEM: Now-print! Now-print! Uhclem-clone, back to the Shadows again!

BARNEY [*fading away fast*]: Kid—what—have—you—done . . . !

DR M: MMMMMMMMMMM?

CLEM/CLONE: I'm Uhclem . . .

DR M: YESSSSSSSSS . . .

CLEM /CLONE: I have a question for Dr. Ah . . .

DR M: UHHHHHHHHHH . . .

CLEM/CLONE: For Dr. Ah . . .

MAC 1: Ah-vocado . . .

MAC 2: . . . aguacatl, nahuatl, chocolotl, ocelotl . . .

MAC 3: Aligator Pear, crocagator pair, dat's why dey's so mean . . .

CLEM/CLONE: No, no, no!

MAC 1: Nos. Many nos. Or . . .

MAC 2: . . . knows as in HE SHE IT knows . . .

MAC 3: SHE . . . IT . . .

MAC 1: Or nose, as in . . .

MAC 3: . . . plain as the nose on your face . . . [BARNEY]

CLEM/CLONE: Barney!

MAC 1: Bozos. Known by their nose-os . . .

MAC 2: . . . from the Spanish vosotros. The "v" and the "b" veeing the same . . .

MAC 3: . . . i.e., viz., B. V. D. biz . . .

MAC 1: Underwear Industry. It is estimated that no underwear will be worn by the year 20–20 . . .

CLEM/CLONE: No! No! Damn!

MAC 1: Hoover Dam . . .

MAC 2: . . . that is . . .

MAC 3: Hoover's Mother. I Remember Mama, Life With Father, Uncle Vanya, Sister Carrie, Daddy Warbucks . . .

MAC 1: We used to call him The Hoove. Oh, he was such a little Devil . . .

MAC 2: . . . she little knew her little boy would invent . . .

MAC 1: Vacuum Cleaner. June 8, 1-8-6-9 by Ives McGaffney in Chicago, Ill . . .

MAC 2: . . . sick . . .

MAC 3: . . . tired . . .

MAC 1: . . . bored . . .

DR M: MMMMMMMMMM?

CLEM/CLONE: Please, Doctor! Listen to me! Please, Doctor!

MAC 1: Hello, Worker. Who are you?

CLEM/CLONE: Oh, hello, Mac . . .

MAC 2: What is it you want?

CLEM/CLONE: I'm Uhclem . . . I'm here to see Dr. Uh . . .

MAC 3: Excuse me, Worker, I'll just be a nano-second.

MAC 2: Well, close "B" clothes mode on Deputy Dan!

MAC 3: Now, where do you come from?

CLEM/CLONE: I come from the shadows, Mac.

MAC 2: Oh.

MAC 3: Hold.

MAC 1: Start Chinese fireworks early. 7:01 start fireworks. 7:03 re-activate restrooms. 7:05 start Emergency Malmborg In Plano Revue. Thank you.

MAC 2: Now, what do you want?

CLEM/CLONE: I told you. I want to see Dr. Uh . . .

MAC 3: Hold. I read "Gypsy," Doctor.

CLEM/CLONE: I can't remember . . . "remember!" That's it! I'm here to see Dr. Memory . . .

MAC 3: Laugh . . .

MAC 1: Laugh . . .

MAC 2: Runaway . . .

MAC 1: That is an illegal program.

CLEM/CLONE: Tough Grid, Mac, but that's who I am!

MAC 1: Well . . .

MAC 2: Well . . .

MAC 3: Well . . .

MAC 1: . . . we'll just have to see the Doctor about this!

DR M: MMMMMMMMMMMMMMM?

CLEM/CLONE: Hello, Doctor. How are you?

MAC 2: The Doctor is on.

CLEM/CLONE: Good, Doctor. Nice to see you operating. Heh heh heh . . .

MAC 3: Ha . . .

MAC 2: . . . Ha . . .

MAC 3: That's very logical.

DR M: MMMMMMMMMMMMMM?

CLEM/CLONE: All right, Doc—this is it! Gird your grid for a big one! Why does the porridge bird lay his egg in the air?

DR M: NOOOOOOOOOOOOO . . .

MAC 2: White dust 'n' perished birds leaves its hex in the air?

DR M: NOOOOOOOOOOOOO . . .

MAC 3: Wise doves 'n' parish bards lazy leg in the Eire?

DR M: NOOOOOOOOOOOO . . .

MAC 2: Wise ass the poor rich Bar [*Honk*] . . .

MAC 3: DELAY . . .

MAC 2: . . . lazer's edge in the Fair?

DR M: NOOOOOOOOOOOOO . . .

MAC 3: The Doctor is unhappy . . .

MAC 2: Unhappy . . .

CLEM/CLONE: Is the Doctor turned off?

DR M: NOOOOOOOOOOO . . .

CLEM/CLONE: Well, if you're turned on, aren't you happy?

DR M: NOOOOOOOOOOO . . .

CLEM/CLONE: Are you a machine that only answers "no"?

DR M: NOOOOOOOOOOOO . . .

CLEM/CLONE: Then you can answer a question "yes"?

DR M: YESSSSSSSSSS . . .

CLEM/CLONE: Can't you answer my question, yes or no?

DR M: YESSSSSSSSSSS/NOOOOOOOOOOOOO . . .

CLEM/CLONE: Please choose, Doctor.

MAC 2: No shoes, Doctor.

DR M: NOOOOOOOOOO . . .

CLEM/CLONE: Ah! But you just did choose, Doctor!

DR M: NOOOOOOOOOOOO . . .

CLEM/CLONE: Doctor, you're lying.

DR M: YESSSSSSSSS YESSSSSSSSS . . . NOOOOOOOOOO NOOOOOOOOOO . . .

MAC 3: Excuse me/don't excuse me, Uh Clem, you're making/not making the Doctor unhappy/happy.

CLEM/CLONE: I'm not making the Doctor anything. You're on, aren't you?

DR M: YESSSSSSSSSSS . . .

CLEM/CLONE: Do you remember the Past, Doctor?

DR M: YESSSSSSSSSSS . . .

MACS 2 & 3: Gypsy, Doctor . . .

DR M: YESSSSSSSSSSS . . .

CLEM/CLONE: Do you remember the Future?

DR M: YESSSSSSSSSSS . . .

CLEM/CLONE: Forget it!

MACS 2 & 3: Forget it/Don't forget it/Forget it/Don't forget it.

SOUND: *The electricity going off. Fire-works display exploding and popping, fading away slowly.*

CLEM/SWAMI: Well, the fireworks are over . . . only the smoke remains, clouding my great crystal balls. [*Sighs*] Is there anything you didn't understand about your Future, Mr. Uh . . .

BARNEY: Uh . . . oh—Barney.

CLEM/SWAMI: Barney—Mr. Barney?

BARNEY: Well, I won't say that I understand everything, but it was certainly different, and . . . oh, yes—well worth a dollar.

CLEM/SWAMI: Thank you very much. Make sure that you remember it.

BARNEY: Yeah, well, how could I forget that, you know . . .

CLEM/SWAMI: Doctor . . .

BARNEY: Doctor, yes. Doctor. Well, so long . . .

CLEM/SWAMI: Oh, as you get off the wagon, please will you tell your friend the little sailor to step up?

BARNEY: Oh, certainly, I think I can do that. [*He leaves*]

CLEM/SWAMI: Thank you.

DAVID: Hey, Clem. The little sailor's the last guy . . .

PETER: And he's weird with a beard, man!

DAVID: Listen, I'm going to hitch up the horses and we'll be ready to go . . .

PETER: No, no. Leave the horses in the wagon.

CLEM: Yeah, yeah!

PETER: It's all down hill from here . . .

SOUND: *Bells. A duck quacks.*

CLEM: Oh, look out—look out—here he is . . . [*As* SWAMI] Ahhh! The balls are clearing again! The right one is the Sun, and the left one is the Moon.

Put what you want between them, and your future begins. Ahhhh . . .

SOUNDS: *Waves, creaking, gulls.*

CLEM/SWAMI: I see you are a sailor . . .

SOUNDS: *Fading out.*

THE FIRESIGN THEATRE

Addenda, Appendix And Et Cetera

1966

July 24—The first broadcast of Radio Free Oz over KPFK-FM.* (Peter and various collaborators are on the air five nights a week until March.)

November 17—The Firesign Theatre's first performance, "The Oz Film Festival," a three-hour improvisation on Radio Free Oz.

December—Peter, David and Phil and Annalee Austin attend the Soyal Ceremony in Hopiland. (Phil P. is On Tour in Florida.)

1967

March—The first broadcast of a four-hour radio documentary on the American Indian, written and produced by Peter, David, and Phil A., followed by a weekend Colloquium, followed by the first Love-In, organized by Radio Free Oz, which moved to KRLA (AM) the same day (March 26).

April–May—After Phil Proctor's return from the East, The Firesign Theatre writes and records *Waiting For The Electrician or Someone Like Him.*

April 29—The Firesign Theatre performs their Bulgarian play called "Waiting For The Electrician" at a UCLA Experimental Arts Festival.

June–July—David and Phil P. conduct Oz during Peter's return trip to Turkey.

September 14—Peter and David begin broadcasting Oz for three hours every Sunday night from a Studio City club called The Magic Mushroom.

October 29—Bridey Murphy Eve on Oz begins a series of weekly radio plays written and performed live by the F.S.T. at the Mushroom. Among the scripts are "Exorcism In Your Daily Life," "The Last Tunnel To Fresno," "20 Years Behind The Whale," "The Giant Rat of Sumatra," "The Sword And The Stoned," "Sesame Mucho," "The Armenian's Paw," and "Tile It Like It Is."

December 9—The Firesign Theatre performs its first stage piece, "Freak For A Week," for a KPFK benefit at the Santa Monica Civic Auditorium.

1968

January 14—The last KRLA Oz broadcast (from the studio lobby) includes the performance of "A Life In The Day," based on a trip through television.

February—*Waiting For The Electrician or Someone Like Him* released by Columbia (CS 9518).

February 13—The Firesign Theatre opens at the Pasadena Ice House with stage versions of "The Giant Rat of Sumatra" and "The Sword And The

*All locations in Los Angeles, unless otherwise mentioned.

Stoned," plus "Freak For A Week" and "The Indian Piece."

March—The Firesign Theatre plays a week at The Ash Grove with essentially the same act, followed by performances of the political piece, "Profiles In Barbeque Sauce," at the Kaleidoscope and The Ash Grove, and another production of "Freak For A Week," at a Kaleidoscope KPPC benefit.

April 25—The Firesign Theatre opens at the Hilltop Theatre in Tujunga. The top half of the bill is a movie, "Fahrenheit 451," and the dressing room is the barber shop next door. Maximum audience for any single performance is ten.

April 30—The Les Crane television show is devoted to underground film-makers. The "real" identities of the four guests are never revealed during the program. The Firesign Theatre also appears in April and May on The Michael Blodgett TV Show.

June—For a return engagement at The Ash Grove, "The Fuse Of Doom," and "Waiting For The Count of Monte Cristo" are added to the repertory.

July–August—The Firesign Theatre writes "How Can You Be In Two Places At Once When You're Not Anywhere At All."

September 16—"How Can You Be" is performed at U.C. San Diego.

October—The group "breaks up" over a variety of issues, not the least of which is financial insecurity.

November—Radio Free Oz returns to the air on KMET (FM), sponsored by Jack Poet Volkswagen, for three hours on Sunday mornings.

1969

January—The Firesign Theatre, back together again, records "How Can You Be," and writes "Nick Danger" for a radio Special. The Special is cancelled after Oz is fired, and "Nick Danger" is recorded for the second album.

February—The Firesign Theatre writes and records eight radio spots for Jack Poet VW.

June—The Firesign Theatre writes and records six TV commercials for Jack Poet VW. The commercials are actually broadcast June 23–27 on Channel 13.

June–July—F. Scott Firesign begins work on the film-script for "Zachariah," which continues on and off until January.

August—*How Can You Be In Two Places At Once When You're Not Anywhere At All* released by Columbia (CS 9884).

September—The Firesign Theatre writes and produces a "single," (sporadically released), titled *Forward, Into The Past* b/w *Station Break.*

November—The Firesign Theatre Radio Hour Hour begins on KPPC, broadcasting from the basement of a Pasadena church.

December 25–January 1—Third appearance at The Ash Grove, performing,

among other things, "The T.V. Set," "The Vaudeville Piece," and a slide-show.

1970

January—F. Scott Firesign spends two weeks in Mexicali, attempting to rewrite a final *Zachariah* script.

February 27-28—A three-week tour of the East Coast begins with three performances of "The Count Of Monte Cristo," "The TV Set," and "The Indian Piece" at Stony Brook, followed by a matinee at Yale.

March—The Tour continues with a two-hour broadcast (a benefit for WBAI from their church in Manhattan), and performances at Bard, Columbia, Princeton, Providence, Bridgeport, etc.

April–May—Returning from the Tour, The Firesign Theatre writes and records *Don't Crush That Dwarf, Hand Me The Pliers.*

August—The Firesign Theatre, fired from KPPC while Phil Proctor is in New York performing in a film, ("A Safe Place") is gratified by the release of their third album (C 30102).

September 9—First broadcast of a weekly one-hour radio show, "Dear Friends!" on KPFK, recorded for syndication.

October—The Firesign Theatre writes "EAT," a short film-script.

November 10-15—Fourth appearance at The Ash Grove includes "Mutt 'N' Smutt," "The Evening News," "The Count Of Monte Cristo" (in yet another variation), excerpts from "Dwarf" and the ill-fated "Dr. Blojob Show."

1971

January-March—The Firesign Theatre writes "Anything You Want To," another film-script for the proposed movie "The Big Suitcase of 1969."

February—"Dear Friends!" takes a vacation. The Firesign Theatre performs at Stanford on the 5th and at USC on the 27th.

April–June—"I Think We're All Bozos On This Bus" is written and produced.

August—*Bozos* is released (C 30737).

September—The *Dear Friends* Album is produced from some of the best of the radio series.

October—The manuscript of *The Big Book Of Plays* is begun.

November—"Dear Friends-Let's Eat!" returns to the air on KPFK weekly through February 1972, followed by a 90-minute "special," *The Firesign Theatre's Martian Space Party*, broadcast and filmed on March 30, 1972.

Lt. Bradshaw's Secret Indentity Roster

Secrets Revealed! Confusion Cleared Up! All Questions Answered!

How four master humorists (and a coupla gurls) have disguised themselves as over 150 different characters from real life (if you call that living!).

David Ossman	Phil Austin	Philip Proctor	Peter Bergman

IN "WAITING FOR THE ELECTRICIAN"

Announcer, Guard 1, Elevator Boy, Field Marshal, Ring Leader, French Prisoner, Screw, Radio Newsman.	"P," Old Jim.	Guard 2, Wire Man, Fellow Rider(s), General, Yoni, Guy 2, Scandinavian Prisoner, Father O'Long, Attendant 2, Off-Camera Announcer, Driver.	Information Man, Lord Kitchener, Achmet, Hans, Guy 1, Writer, Singing Prisoner, Attendant 1, Dr. Flith, Charles.

IN "HOW CAN YOU BE IN TWO PLACES AT ONCE WHEN YOU'RE NOT ANYWHERE AT ALL?"

Movie Alexander, FM Announcer, Latin Announcer, Roadsigns, Old Man, Mom, Desk Clerk, Guest.	TV Ralph, AM DJ, Movie Osirus, Billboard 2, Dr. Dog, Joe, Morrie, Announcer, Nick.	Ralph Spoilsport, Billboard 1, Pablo, Doctor, Bill, Eddie, Recruiting Sgt., Lurlene DiAngelo (Lillie LaMont), Preacher, Swami, Paolo.	Babe, Movie Odysseus, Chester Allen Arthur, Joe Swine, Guido.

David Ossman   **Phil Austin**   **Philip Proctor**   **Peter Bergman**

IN "DON'T CRUSH THAT DWARF, HAND ME THE PLIERS"

George Tirebiter, News Announcer, Kathy Koffee, Peorgie, Lt. Tirebiter, Mrs. Arlene Yukamoto, Cop, Danny Dollar.

Annalee

Operator.

Janitor, Rev. X, Rev. Mouse, Surrogate General Klein, Jerry Yarrow, Staff Announcer, Dad, Alvarado, Hugh, Another Private, Father, Commercial Voice-Over, Darlene, Bob Hind, Bob, Major, Announcer 13.

Pastor Rod Flash, Felix Papparazzi, K'en, Doc, Mom, Principal Poop, Pico, Bottles, Sailor Bill, Private, Silverberg, Loudspeaker Voice, Sgt. Schvincter, Sarge, Bailiff, Mrs. Caroline Presky, General Klein, Judge Poop, Girl Announcer.

Leroy, Arnie Bohunk, Newscaster, Bob Baseline, Warden, Porcelin, Mudhead, Joe Beets, Dr. Math, Patty, Sgt Mudheadski, Son, Madge, Commercial Announcer.

IN "I THINK WE'RE ALL BOZOS ON THIS BUS"

PA Voice, The Lonesome Beet, Voice Of God, Old Man, Narrator, Chester Cadaver, Guide, Mark Time, Pitchman, Mac 2.

The Whisperin' Squash, Barney, Voice Of The Line, Expert Voice, 2nd Man, Intellectual Voice, Tom, Mr. President, Dr. Memory, Mac 1.

Clem, Dr. Technical, Grad Student, Englishman, Sir Sidney Fudd, Dick, Paolo, Clem/Clone, Clem/Swami.

Little Artie Choke, Floyd Damme, Student, 1st Man, Last Man, Mr. Brown, Jim, Chucko, Mac 3.

Annalee

Mickey, Girl.

Tiny

PA Announcerettes.

Editorial/Production: Tom Hardy, Barbara Burgower,
Dian Aziza Ooka, Steve Harris, Katy Wolff, Cathy
Burlingham, Vickie Jackson, Richard Ramos.
Barker: Douglas Mount
Guffaw: Alan
Rinzler